THE EFFECTIVENESS OF POLICING

The Effectiveness of Policing

edited by

R. V. G. CLARKE

and

J. M. HOUGH

Home Office Research Unit

Gower

Published by

Gower Publishing Company Limited,
Westmead, Farnborough, Hants., England.

The effectiveness of policing

   1   Police—Research
   I   Clarke, Ronald Victor Germuseus
   II   Hough, J. M.

  363.2   HV7923

ISBN 0 566 00297 3

Printed in Great Britain by
Biddles Ltd, Guildford, Surrey

Contents

Tables

Foreword

Any organisation that spends a lot of someone else's money is under an obligation to check that it is spending it to best effect. Companies which utilise an advancing technology, or which cater to a changing market, regularly allocate a significant proportion of their budgets to research on product development, consumer response and market conditions. Since these considerations also apply to policing, it would be reasonable to expect at least 1 per cent of the police budget to be devoted to research. Given that the total police budget of England and Wales for 1978 was about £1,200 million, and given that research on police effectiveness has only started in the last decade, these are excellent grounds for authorising a substantial, but cautious expansion.

The expansion needs to be cautious because there are doubts about the effectiveness of research as well as the effectiveness of policing, and we have much to learn about the most effective ways of organising research. It is to be expected that a variety of persons and bodies will be interested in research of various kinds that involve the police, so it would be to no-one's advantage to create a comprehensive arrangement for co-ordinating research, but within the particular field of studies on police effectiveness there are definite problems concerning the initiation, administration and utilisation of research. Who is to decide which issues are to be investigated? How are police and research personnel to be associated in guiding the research while it is in progress? How are the findings to be utilised and by whom? Are they, in the British context, to be used in deciding the resources to be allocated to the police? Are they to be fed into the police service, through training, promotion, examination and selection procedures? In Great Britain at present there is no shared understanding about who is to accumulate new knowledge on various aspects of policing, how they are to be rewarded for it, and how that knowledge can best be passed on. This is reflected in the uncertainty about whether a university degree in police studies should be instituted, and, if it were, how it should be related to the structure of career advancement in the police. It is reflected in the absence of a quality professional journal which, of course, is related to the paucity of persons who could contribute articles of the kind desired and the doubts about whether it would be in their career interests to devote their energies to doing so. It is reflected in the discussions about the role of the Police Staff College at Bramshill. In 1973 the editor of *The Police Journal* wrote:

> The post of Commandant of the Police College, Bramshill, is vacant again. The governing body have invited applications from a wide field and it seems very likely that those who apply from within the Service will be much outnumbered by laymen.
>
> This at first sight is incongruous. The College has been training middle and senior ranking police officers for a quarter of a century. Are too few of such people and of the chief officers who did not attend Bramshill courses sufficiently qualified for the job? The answer is, of course, that there are plenty of serving officers who could hold it with distinction. The reason for the paucity of applications from them lies in the peculiar structure of the Service and the position of chief officers. If the police were nationalized (we hope they never will be) it would be easy to *post* a senior officer to the College, with the understanding as at, say, the Staff College, Camberley, that after his spell there he would be given some advantageous move. No such guarantee can be given in the police, though it is a good sign that both the outgoing Commandant and his predecessor left the College on appointment as Assistant Commissioners of Police of the Metropolis.
>
> Ideally, the Service thinks, the post should be filled by an outstanding police officer for whom his time as Commandant would be followed by a return to high operational responsibility. The Commandant's post is the key post in the Service's higher training: that goes without saying: but it is also a unique opportunity for the man who holds it to gain an overall view of the police and to add immeasurably to his own professional qualifications. In that sense it would be a great pity if the post went to anyone but a policeman. (*The Police Journal*, 1973, 46, pp. 106-7)

A police officer's career prospects depend upon decisions made in the 43 police forces of England and Wales, not upon the Home Office or the Staff College. If new knowledge about police effectiveness is to be obtained and utilised, this will require a widely based appreciation of the part that can be played by research and an improved link between research and higher training.

Before discussing the findings of research it could be helpful to reflect upon the two chief terms that give this book its title: effectiveness and policing. Notice that the book is about policing rather than about police, and that there is an ambiguity, for 'policing' can denote both the activities of a body of uniformed men, a constabulary, and a feature of any organised activity whatsoever. It is perfectly acceptable to talk of professional bodies, like those of lawyers, doctors and architects, as self-policing. Whenever people stand in a queue in a cafeteria they commit themselves to a social norm and indicate to the would-be queue-jumper that he is expected to do likewise. An element of policing is built into any patterned activity. This is relevant to the assessment of effectiveness, for it could well be assumed that a constabulary is most effective when crime is lowest, but crime may be low for reasons that have nothing to do with the constabulary. It might therefore be helpful to represent some of these factors in a simple diagram, (see below).

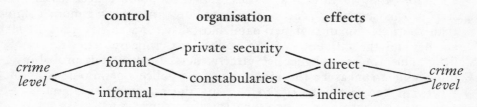

The level of crime is influenced both by the informal social controls based upon acquaintance, neighbourhood and shared values, and upon the formal controls of supervision and legal sanctions. Formal controls are operated both by the constabularies and by a variety of special purpose enforcement bodies, some of which, like store detectives, make substantial contributions to the figures of recorded crime. The activities of the constabularies, like those of private security bodies, have direct effects in deterring particular offenders and detecting others, but the constabularies also, by their demeanour and their contacts with citizens, reinforce public notions of propriety and the informal controls of society. Both these direct and indirect effects are related to crime levels. This book focuses on a small part of the wider picture, upon the direct effects of the activities of the primary police forces, or constabularies, and it considers these apart from the operations of the courts and corrections systems although these are obviously of central importance to the control of crime and the maintenance of order.

The word 'effectiveness' also calls for comment. It is neatly distinguished from efficiency at the beginning of the essay by David Farmer, but that distinction may be too concise for some readers. To distinguish the effectiveness of policing from the efficiency of particular methods of policing, they may find it helpful to draw a comparison with a very different field, that of the maternity services. Ante-natal clinics are held to reduce peri-natal mortality; their effectiveness can be assessed by the extent to which the figures of infant and maternal deaths are reduced. But similar reductions might be achieved by different methods and the cheaper the method the more efficient would it be. The effectiveness of policing cannot so easily be assessed in the same way because while nearly all peri-natal deaths are recorded, the figures of recorded crime are too unreliable to use for such a purpose. The motivations of people when they define an action as criminal are more complex than those of people who report a death. As Keith Bottomley and Clive Coleman explain in their article, actions regarded as criminal have first to be discovered, then reported and then recorded before they feature in statistics, and their number declines at each step in this sequence. The determinants of crime are far more complex than the determinants of peri-natal mortality, and so many of them are beyond the influence of the police that crime statistics are of little value for assessing police effectiveness. Indeed, it is probably impossible to measure the effectiveness of police operations as a whole. What can be done is to try to measure the effectiveness of one activity, like patrol, in controlling specific crimes, such as street robbery.

It should also be possible to measure the relative efficiency of different ways of utilising resources. In any British police force certain numbers of men will be engaged on criminal investigation, criminal intelligence and crime prevention. It should be possible to measure the effects of changing the numbers employed on these duties in order to determine optimum manpower allocation. To do so will require the development of more sophisticated accounting techniques, and these should find a place in any programme on research into police effectiveness.

Most research starts up as an extension of an ongoing programme in a university, a commercial company or a government establishment. Police research cannot fit snugly within any single institution. It must relate to police forces, governmental bodies and to the universities. It must draw upon several specialisms. Its main problems are not those of money, but of building a community of imaginative and enthusiastic research workers who can collaborate in developing the potentialities of a body of good ideas. This community must look both inwards and outwards, for everyone knows how an administrator is likely to respond to a research worker who talks only in jargon and cannot communicate with the man on the job. A necessary element in future research, at any rate in Britain, is for research workers to analyse the way members of the public, and police officers themselves, think about policing, so as to make explicit the many implicit propositions. Only when these assumptions are dragged out and clearly formulated will it be possible to identify the alternatives and to spot ways of comparing the effectiveness of different policies. Only then will research workers and police officers be able to communicate effectively with one another.

Faced with more demands for service than they can meet, the police in Britain wonder what their role should now be. How far should they act as uniformed social workers? How far are they bound to act as a repressive force? It is easy to misrepresent this self-questioning by highlighting the opposite poles and playing down the fundamental agreement that in some circumstances the police always have undertaken social functions while in other circumstances they are always obliged to be firm in maintaining public order. Partly, of course, this is a matter of public image, but when the police enjoy a favourable image their tasks are made much easier. It would be folly for the police to accept the romantic image of the television scene and to allow the public to regard them as responsible, almost unaided, for combating crime. That is a struggle they could never win. Yet what sort of image should they foster instead? What should they put in place of what the editors of this book characterise as 'the rational/deterrent model'? That is another question which cannot at present be answered. It would first be necessary to identify and analyse the alternatives, encompassing both the psychological dimension of how people think about their societies and the more practical dimension of cause and effect in day to day operations. The latter will entail the painstaking construction of sophisticated models of the interrelations between the various police activities and other parts of society, setting out all the connections and the ways in which one element influences each other. Such models will look far more complicated than a wiring diagram for a television set, but that is only to be expected since society is so much more complicated.

A research worker always benefits from discussion with a group of peers who understand what he is trying to do and can criticise his proposals, procedures and interpretations. Research on police effectiveness often has to be intensive over a period of many months, because circumstances change over time and this makes it the more difficult to draw inferences from changes in crime rates and similar measures. The social scientist who holds a university teaching position is often poorly placed to manage the sort of research conducted by George Kelling in Kansas City. It will therefore not be surprising if most of the research on police effectiveness is carried out by professional research agencies either within government or relying upon government sponsorship. But if there is to be a research community to stimulate and assist the investigator, the participation of academics and of serving police officers is essential. If the research worker is to appreciate the cultural dimension of his material (always important in

xi

this field since ideas about law, morality and enforcement are central to all human cultures), and if he is to question practices which are taken for granted in his own country, he needs the support of an international research community. The different national backgrounds of the participants in the Cambridge conference, and of the contributors to this book, show that such an international community exists in embryo.

Michael Banton

University of Bristol
July 1979

Contributors

Michael Banton	Professor, Department of Sociology, University of Bristol.
A. K. Bottomley	Senior Lecturer in Criminology, Department of Social Administration, University of Hull.
R. V. G. Clarke	Senior Principal Research Officer, Home Office Research Unit, London.
C. A. Coleman	Lecturer in Sociology, Department of Social Administration, University of Hull.
Peter Engstad	Chief, Law Enforcement Research, Research Division, Ministry of the Solicitor-General of Canada, Ottawa.
John L. Evans	Chief, Causes and Prevention Research, Research Division, Ministry of the Solicitor-General of Canada, Ottawa.
David J. Farmer	Director, Police Division, National Institute of Law Enforcement and Criminal Justice, Washington DC.
Peter W. Greenwood	Criminal Justice Programme Director, Rand Corporation, Santa Monica, California.
J. M. Hough	Senior Research Officer, Home Office Research Unit, London.
George L. Kelling	Evaluation Field Staff Director, Police Foundation, Washington DC.
Peter K. Manning	Professor, Departments of Sociology and Psychiatry, Michigan State University, East Lansing, Michigan.

Tony Pate   Senior Researcher, Police Foundation,
                         Newark, New Jersey.

D. W. Steenhuis   Head, Research and Documentation Centre,
                         Ministry of Justice, The Hague, Netherlands.

Mary Ann Wycoff   Senior Researcher, Police Foundation,
                         Madison, Wisconsin.

1 Introduction

J. M. Hough and R. V. G. Clarke

The background to the workshop

This book comprises a number of papers prepared for a workshop on police effectiveness which was held at Cambridge in the summer of 1979. The workshop formed part of the biennial criminological conference organised by the Cambridge Institute of Criminology and was convened at the invitation of the Institute by the editors of this book, who are members of the Home Office Research Unit. The workshop theme—police effectiveness in dealing with crime—reflects some of the research interests of the Research Unit. The Unit undertakes criminological research and other research in the social sciences, and also manages a programme of funded research in universities and other institutions. It has only recently begun to undertake research on the police, and is not the only Home Office department engaged on police research: the Police Scientific Development Branch is a somewhat larger research organisation, orientated towards the provision of scientific and technological solutions to operational problems defined by the police. The Research Unit has a tradition of evaluative research, mainly in the context of penal treatment, and it was decided that issues of effectiveness would also provide a valuable, but not exclusive, focus for its research on the police. Other work in progress is concerned with police/race relations and with police interrogation practice.

There has been little evaluative research on police effectiveness carried out in Britain, and this is reflected in the variety of nationalities of authors contributing to this book. The workshop was intended to publicise their findings and to encourage more researchers in this country—criminologists in particular—to follow their lead. In that police research is not always properly informed by an understanding of crime, there seems a particular role for criminologists to play in this area. And many criminologists would probably be attracted by the issues requiring further research, for example the need identified in the chapter by Kelling and his colleagues for more detailed descriptive studies of police behaviour.

1

The rational deterrent model of policing

To the 'man in the street' the concept of effective policing is unproblematic: effective policing is achieved when the police succeed in bringing criminals to book. But such clarity of vision is a form of myopia, as police administrators and researchers are increasingly recognising. Previously well-attested yardsticks of police performance are now heavily questioned, and policing theory is more immediately concerned with the process of re-mapping the limits of police capabilities and responsibilities.

Perhaps this discussion can best be anchored by outlining the conventional—and questionable—set of assumptions against which the effectiveness of policing is too often assessed. This can be characterised as the 'rational/deterrent model' of policing, and its main elements can be listed as:

1 The police are the primary agents of social control.
2 Social control can be equated with the control of crime, which thus constitutes the primary objective of the police.
3 The content of police work is primarily crime-orientated.
4 Crime is committed by a small number of individuals whose selfishly motivated behaviour threatens society.
5 The main strategies available to the police are those of deterrence.
6 The police are organised as a rational bureaucracy: police administrators assess the best crime fighting strategies, and implement these through a paramilitary chain of command.

Some caveats should be stated about this model. Positing models involves formalisation and simplification of the assumptions which people make about the world. Assumptions may be explicitly expressed, in which case they are easily accessible to outsiders; but these are not necessarily the ones which guide action. The assumptions which *do* guide action may only be implicit in action. Thus the status of a model can be ambiguous—it may be a description of explicit viewpoints, or it may amount to an interpretive account of action. The rational/deterrent model of policing comprises those assumptions explicit in the popular press and in the public pronouncements of police administrators and, partly as a consequence, the assumptions held implicitly by the 'man in the street'. It does not necessarily comprise the assumptions either implicit or explicit, held by police officers 'on the ground'; but it underpins to some extent the dominant administrative theory of policing, in the sense that the rationale for many administrative decisions is provided by the model. But if it pretended in any way to be an adequate representation of police administrators' assumptions, it would be a distorted over-simplification—a 'straw man'.

A moment's reflection will show that the model is a quite inadequate description of the *totality* of police work, which comprises a multiplicity of tasks both related and unrelated to crime. The police for example provide a 'front-line' response to natural and man-made disasters such as floods and traffic accidents. They are responsible for crowd control at public occasions, and the maintenance of public order at demonstrations, football matches and so on; and of course the maintenance of public order may be regarded as a form of crime-prevention, even if the assaults and acts of vandalism which the police aim to prevent are not always regarded as 'crime' in the public eye. Again, considerable police resources are devoted to the enforcement of traffic legislation—another area of the law not usually equated with 'crime'. The rational/deterrent model takes little account of other aspects of policing—the non-criminal 'social service' work; community and schools liaison; and the provision of crime-prevention advice. It implies the centrality to police work of strategies such as detective work, fast response to calls for police assistance and preventive patrolling—both routine uniformed patrol and more specialised patrolling methods. It contains straightforward policing objectives, and yields apparently straightforward criteria of effectiveness and efficiency: if crime levels remain within acceptable limits, the police are effective, and if this is achieved with acceptable expenditure, they are efficient. If crime levels rise beyond acceptable levels, the police are ineffective, either because they have inadequate resources, or because they use available resources inefficiently.

Given that the rational/deterrent model is a transparently inadequate description of police work, why is so much emphasis placed on it in this discussion? In the first place, we would argue, it informs public expectations of the police; and if the police are held accountable for crime control they will inevitably attach priority to this function. Moreover the model constitutes the 'backdrop' of assumptions against which political discussions about police resources are conducted; the rationale most often advanced for increasing police resources is that crime would thus be held in check. And finally, though no senior police officers would give such a bald rendering of the complexities of policing, the model nonetheless casts questions about police effectiveness *in dealing with crime* in a mould recognisably that of police administration. These questions are seen as *technical* questions; administrators want to know, for example, what is the best balance of resources between investigative and patrolling strategies; whether traditional uniformed patrol is as effective as specialised patrolling techniques; what constitutes optimum levels of patrol, and so on.

Research on police effectiveness

If research on police effectiveness is defined narrowly as research addressed to these questions, then most work has been undertaken in the United States; this in part reflects the fact that the 'research industry' is better developed there than elsewhere, but there are also more specific origins to this body of work. In the mid-1960s President Johnson set up the President's Crime Commission, marking a declaration of a 'war on crime'. Whilst indicating that it would not be easy to win this war, the Commission expressed confidence in its report (President's Commission, 1967) that victory was possible, given sufficient resources. The technocratic approach of the Commission was very much in line with the rational/deterrent model of policing set out above. Following the Commission's report the Omnibus Crime Control and Safe Streets Act was passed in 1968, and the Law Enforcement Assistance Administration's National Institute of Law Enforcement and Criminal Justice was established: as Farmer explains in his chapter the LEAA has funded a very extensive programme of research, much of it on the police, including evaluative studies and work in the tradition of operations research. Research on police effectiveness received further impetus in 1970, with the establishment of the Police Foundation, an independent research organisation, which has either sponsored or itself undertaken a wide range of research on police effectiveness.

After a decade of such research it is now possible to detect emergent trends. The most significant of these—one which receives attention in every chapter in this book—is that it is difficult to detect precisely what effects the various police deterrent strategies have on crime. Experimental research on the deterrent effects of routine uniformed patrol suggests that at least in the short term, changes in patrol levels have little or no effect on crime (e.g. Bright, 1969; Kelling et al., 1974; Schnelle et al., 1975, 1977). Evaluations of specialist patrolling strategies are equivocal. Some successes are reported (see for example Boydstun, 1975; Halper and Ku, 1975; Pate et al., 1976) but the strategies often appear to have unintended and unacceptable consequences on, for example, community relations. As Farmer's paper describes, it now seems clear that the two studies (NYPD, 1955; Chaiken et al., 1974) most quoted in support of patrolling effectiveness were subject to 'data-rigging' by the police.

The reasons for these findings may lie in the nature of the crime itself. Studies of the way in which crimes become known to the police show that the likelihood of a uniformed officer on routine patrol intercepting a crime in progress is very small; for example, it was estimated in the report of the President's Crime Commission that a patrol officer in a large American city could expect to intercept a street robbery in progress once every fourteen years (President's Commission, 1967). Whilst the aggregated crime statistics seem to represent an overwhelming problem, the number of incidents is really very small if account is taken of the number of opportunities for crime inherent in the activities of a huge population of citizens for the twenty-four hours of the day. For instance, each household in Britain will be burgled on average once every 35 years—assuming that is, that around twice as many burglaries occur as are reported to the police. And these relatively few incidents are distributed over an extensive geographical area; an average foot beat in a large British city covers in the region of 200 acres, 4—5 miles of public roadway, and a population of about 4,000, while a mobile beat is three times the size. Moreover, much crime takes place in private and that which occurs in public is often accomplished quickly, stealthily and without warning. The chances of the police witnessing or being in a position to intervene in such events are therefore tiny and so in the great majority of cases they are likely to be faced with the much more difficult and time-consuming problems of investigation.

The validity of fast response as a deterrent strategy has been largely undermined by studies such as that of the Kansas City Police Department (1978): this showed that any improvement in response time is highly unlikely to produce more arrests, as in the vast majority of cases the first recourse of people who have been victimised, very understandably, is to seek comfort and advice from friends and neighbours, and only after a considerable period—between 20 and 40 minutes on average—do they call the police. Thus only very rarely do the police receive calls where the speed of response can affect the probability of arrest.

The effectiveness of criminal investigation strategies has also been called into question; Greenwood's study for example suggested that differences in CID organisation and methods are unrelated to variations in crime rates, arrest rates and clearance rates (Greenwood et al., 1977). These findings receive some support from research of a less experimental nature conducted in Britain. Woodley's (1976) analysis of almost 1,500 detected crimes found that 22 per cent of detections followed arrests made at or near the scene of the crime. Fourteen per cent resulted from unequivocal indentification (by name or vehicle number) provided by victims or witnesses, and a further 8 per cent from information provided by victims or others. Twenty per cent of the detections resulted from admissions made by people charged with other offences (the so-called 'offences taken into consideration' or 'TICs'). There are some methodological shortcomings to this research, and the figures should be treated with caution. The data presented by Bottomley and Coleman in this book paint a similar picture. Zander's (1979) small-scale study of defendants at the Old Bailey found that in 38 per cent of the cases the police knew the identity of the offender from the outset. Steer's (in preparation) study of serious crime found that about half of detected crime offenders were detained, arrested or identified at the scene of the crime and that a quarter were cleared up as 'TICs'. All these studies emphasise that most detections are of a routine nature and that detectives are heavily dependent both on information readily available at the scene of the crime and on admissions by offenders already charged with other offences. Only a small proportion of crimes are detected by those procedures typically thought to comprise 'real detective work'—that is the sifting of forensic evidence, the methodical elimination of suspects, and the use of informants. This is not to deny the police are often successful in solving crimes of spectacular outrage, and in containing the level of serious (and rare) crimes such as bank robberies, committed by skilled professional criminals; but a very large amount of detective effort is invested in these crimes. Even if investigative resources were greatly increased, the overall detection rate would in all likelihood be only marginally affected. If around 25 per cent of indictable crimes *cleared up* are detected by 'real detective work', these account for about 10 per cent of indictable crimes *known to the police* (assuming a 40 per cent clear-up rate), and only 2.5 per cent of *all* indictable crimes (assuming that at the very most around a quarter of indictable crimes are reported to the police and subsequently recorded).

Individually these studies are all open to varying degrees of methodological criticism: see, for example, Larson's (1975) critique of the Kansas City Preventive Patrolling Experiment, and that by Gates and Knowles (1976) of Greenwood's study. But collectively they offer a convincing challenge to policing orthodoxy, and their conclusions can be couched in two ways: either the police are less effective than has traditionally been assumed, or else the wrong objectives are being set for the police. In deciding which of these alternatives is more plausible, one has to examine the validity of the policing model which underlies the conventionally agreed set of police objectives.

Shortcomings of the rational/deterrent model

The research reviewed above calls into question the effectiveness of conventional police strategies of deterrence. It suggests that the allocation of even substantially more resources to these strategies would achieve at best a marginal impact on crime. But this is not to suggest that the police are functionless in relation to crime. The experience of some—but by no means all—police strikes shows that an absence

6

or reduction of police may lead to widespread theft, looting, robbery and disorder. Nor is it to suggest that the criminal justice process as a whole has no deterrent effects. Rather, the police do not discharge the function of crime-control which the rational/deterrent model ascribes to them; and further research suggests that the police could never discharge this function. Much of this latter research has been conducted in Britain—and incidentally has been undertaken largely by sociologists rather than criminologists. Although one should remain aware of the dangers of extrapolating from one country to another, the following brief review has a secondary purpose of demonstrating the mutual relevance of research undertaken on both sides of the Atlantic.

In the first place, a number of studies have shown that the police are mainly dependent on the public for information about crime. Reiss' (1971) study found that 87 per cent of crimes known to the police in one American city were reported by members of the public. Coleman and Bottomley's (1976) research in this country yielded an almost identical figure of 86 per cent. McCabe and Sutcliffe (1978) and Mawby (1979) report similar findings. Moreover, victim surveys in the United States, Britain and Europe all demonstrate that a large amount of crime goes unreported. For example, only about 10 per cent of crimes identified by a victim survey conducted in London (Sparks et al., 1977) were in fact recorded by the police. Clearly the police cannot be expected to make much impact on crime when the amount of information at their disposal about crime is so limited.

Secondly, studies documenting the work of the police have shown clearly that a very large proportion of police time is devoted to matters either unrelated to crime or marginally related to crime-fighting objectives. Research conducted in Britain (Punch and Naylor, 1973; McCabe and Sutcliffe, 1978; Comrie and Kings, 1965; Hough, in preparation) has confirmed American findings (e.g. Cumming et al., 1965; Reiss, 1971) that the majority of incidents attended by patrols are non-criminal and that only a very small proportion of incidents result in arrests for crime. Thus Hough's study found that only around a third of calls for police assistance in a Glasgow police division were related to crime (and this includes reports of 'suspect persons' and activations of automatic alarm systems). Crime reports were filed in rather less than half of these incidents, and arrests made in very few indeed. Also, British research on the CID (e.g. Martin and Wilson, 1969; Crust, 1975) has indicated, as did Greenwood's study, that the proportion of time which detectives devote to investigation is rather small. Thus a predominantly 'crime fighting' orientation is not reflected in the work actually undertaken by either the uniformed or investigative branches of the police.

Finally the validity of the rational/deterrent model has been questioned by studies of police organisation, which undermine the picture of police forces as rationally organised bureaucracies engaged in the pursuit of strategies of any sort. Studies set in this country (Cain, 1973; Chatterton, 1979; Holdaway, 1977; Manning, 1977) and in the States (Wilson, 1968; Bittner, 1967; Goldstein, J., 1960; Goldstein, H., 1977; Manning, 1977; Skolnick, 1966; Rubinstein, 1973) and elsewhere (Punch, 1979a, 1979b) all portray a remarkably consistent picture of the extensive autonomy of personnel 'on the ground'. As Wilson observed, 'The police department has the special property ... that within it discretion increases as one moves *down* the hierarchy'. The nature of constables' work is such that they are isolated from effective monitoring and can control the upward flow of information to their superiors. Cain's description, in the sixties, of 'easing' (the avoidance of boredom through unauthorised activities) is confirmed by later studies. Holdaway for example, suggests that the advent of technology—cars and radios—has extended the autonomy of patrol officers, and increased the range of hedonistic pursuits open to them; opportunities for 'action'—fast driving and incidents involving violence—are sought out, while other more routine incidents tend to be avoided. Chatterton in his study of the use of arrest powers argues (as does Bittner) that these are employed less as part of the law enforcement strategies and more as a resource for peace-keeping; and the reasons for invoking powers of arrest lie more in the immediate situational constraints on patrol officers than in 'policy'—an argument advanced in America by Friedrich (1977). Manning's (1977) book *Police Work* and his paper in this book examine in more detail the limitations in interpreting police activity as determined by a paramilitary structure of authority. In general, this group of findings strongly suggests that the extent to which police administrators control their organisations is more limited than the rational/deterrent model implies.

In summary, when one considers not only the research which bears directly on police effectiveness, but also that which is concerned with the content and organisational aspects of police work, the evidence is strong that the capability of the police to affect levels of crime through deterrent strategies is limited. By the same token, it would seem unwise for the police either to claim or accept the objectives of crime control which are popularly ascribed to them.

Alternative conceptions of policing

The rational/deterrent model of policing is both descriptive and pre-scriptive—it constitutes a picture both of how policing works and how it should work in relation to crime. But it fails to take account of the fact that the police are a subsystem of the criminal justice system, which itself is a subsystem of a highly complex system of social control—moral, economic, religious, etc.—which impinges on people's action. Our standards of social behaviour are conventional rather than absolute, and the process by which these conventions are negotiated and maintained is not altogether rational. It also in-adequately recognises that police systems have, as described by Manning (1977), first a dramatic capability—that is, they can create and sustain an appearance which is at odds with 'reality'—and second-ly, a symbolising capability.

The police, in Manning's phrase, are involved in the 'dramatic management of the appearance of effectiveness'. If they can sustain the credibility of the rational/deterrent model, popular belief in their ability to control crime will be self-fulfilling. At a different level, what the police do, or appear to do, symbolises and affirms aspects of the social and moral order. By their presence alone the police symbolise the presence of the state in everyday life—they render explicit the state's interest in the maintenance of order. In so far as their integrity is unquestioned, they symbolise the congru-ence of moral values with those of the state and those inherent in the criminal law. They thus legitimate the state's interest in maintain-ing order, and its monopoly in the use of coercive force. The con-tinuity and stability of the moral order is symbolised by the ritual-istic and ceremonial aspects of police work.

Recognition of the dramatic and symbolising capabilities of the police provides a starting point for a description of the way in which police organisations are located within broader systems of social control. But it is not clear that such description yields prescriptions for policing; there are limits both of desirability and practicability in exploiting the dramatic and symbolic functions of the police. There are obvious political dilemmas in policing by legerdemain. Further-more, public belief in the (relative) effectiveness of the police may be self-fulfilling, but there may be social costs to be reckoned in the 'crime drama'. The popular image of the police battling with an almost intractable crime problem is arguably the main source of people's fear of crime—a fear justified neither by the risks nor by the nature of the vast bulk of crime.

The alternative approaches to policing discussed below have in common a descriptive assumption—that the police have a limited capability for crime control—and a prescriptive assumption—that the police should not claim nor foster a belief in this capability. The first of these approaches would see the police role in relation to crime not as that of law enforcement, nor even of prevention, but primarily as one of servicing the criminal justice machinery. It is premised on the view that crime is the product of structural inequalities (of wealth, education and so on), and that the sort of social intervention needed to achieve an impact on crime lies outside of the remit of police administration. The requirements of the police in pursuing this approach would be first that they are responsive to citizen demands for access to the criminal justice process and secondly that they are responsive to the requirements of 'due process'. In many ways this position mirrors the 'justice' approach to the treatment of offenders, which is being increasingly advocated in response to the apparent ineffectiveness of the criminal justice process in deterring or rehabilitating those who pass through it. It would see the machinery of justice as a necessary evil, and the proper aims of its administrators as the minimisation of harm rather than the maximisation of benefit.

Such a minimal approach to policing is likely to be unpalatable to many people, and may well be over-pessimistic. Moreover, it is based on a view of crime as a phenomenon the definition of which is unproblematic; but most people who ask for police assistance present them not with a 'crime' to be processed, but with a problem to be resolved. A form of elaboration of the first approach consists in a 'service orientation' to police organisation. As Bottomley and Coleman observe in their chapter, the response of many police forces to doubts about their crime fighting objectives has been to adopt secondary objectives of public reassurance and public satisfaction. These secondary objectives are not necessarily seen as instrumental to crime fighting objectives, but may be seen as ends in themselves. Thus according to the service approach, police effectiveness is assessed by the perceived quality of police response to demands made by the public, and law enforcement is regarded simply as one of several resources available to the police in delivering adequate service. Kelling's chapter draws attention to some of the problems inherent in this: public expectations of the police—and thus their satisfaction with the police—are based on a limited awareness of the problems and costs of delivering various levels of service. Moreover the police are very often involved in conflict between individuals or groups. Resolution of the conflict may well be to the satisfaction of one side at the expense of the other, so that 'public satisfaction' alone cannot usually provide a rationale for police action. As Farmer argues in his chapter, there is a need to reassess both the objectives of the 'service' work of the police and the way in which this work is handled.

Perhaps a more constructive response to the limitations of police crime controlling capabilities is to redistribute policing responsibilities so as to match capabilities better. This position is advocated in several chapters of this book; the suggested ways of doing this overlap at a number of points, and all have at root the idea that the main resource for crime prevention lies not with the police, but with the community.

Engstad and Evans advocate a highly eclectic approach to *specific* crime problems; this 'crime specific' or 'situational' approach builds on research undertaken in a more general context of crime prevention (e.g. Reppetto, 1974; Clarke, 1978; Mayhew et al., 1979). It consists of a detailed analysis of the way in which particular crimes in particular places occur; from this an assessment is made of the ways in which situational inducements and environmental opportunities to commit crime can be reduced, and of the extent to which specific organisations and individuals can be held responsible for these reductions. According to the crime specific approach the police have both a catalytic function in encouraging and persuading others to take crime prevention measures, and a substantive function in undertaking preventive strategies themselves.

There are very few examples of the application of the crime specific approach in this country, and there is a need for much more experimentation. Engstad and Evans provide two case histories of seemingly successful implementation in Canada, and a third, described by Heywood (1979), may serve as further illustration. Police in a Canadian city were continually being called to one of a chain of 'quick serve' restaurants to deal with fights, assaults on staff, muggings and so on. Closer analysis of the problem by the police showed that the firm had introduced its standard design of restaurant into an inappropriate environment. No allowance had been made for the high proportion of youths who used the restaurant late at night: when trouble arose the management simply called the police. The police entered into negotiations with the restaurant firm, which led to the employment of greater numbers of more experienced staff in the late evenings, and to the installation of better lighting in the restaurant car park. Trouble at the restaurant then became less frequent.

The crime-specific approach clearly overlaps with the traditional 'physical crime prevention' work of the police, but differs at key points. The latter mainly involves the provision of a limited range of advice about physical security, which the recipient may accept or reject. It may also consist of a limited amount of informal analysis of events which regularly result in disorder; this has led to some successful prevention; liaison with football clubs, for example, has led to closer supervision of football supporters *en route* to the ground

11

and reduced opportunities for disruption. The crime specific approach places considerably more emphasis on formal analysis of problems, and thus requires a greater analytic capability on the part of the police. It also requires a level of negotiating skill beyond that which is normally required of crime prevention officers; it aims not simply to provide advice, but to ensure that this is implemented.

The main theoretical problem highlighted by the crime specific approach is that of 'displacement'—though most other forms of preventive policing are also beset by it. Critics would argue that opportunity-reducing measures aimed at specific crimes may reduce the level of the 'target crime' but will also displace criminal activity to unprotected areas or to other forms of crime. It seems, however, that the likelihood of displacement may have been considerably overestimated and in giving it proper consideration an understanding of particular forms of crime as well as the individuals involved is needed. Highly diverse forms of behaviour are masked by the labels of legal categories, such as robbery, burglary, theft, shoplifting and so on. Even within fairly specific offence groups some offences will be heavily dependent on the temptations and opportunities of the situations in which offenders find themselves, and these can probably be reduced by protecting individual targets. Others within the same offence categories may not so easily be reduced by protecting particular targets, even though the targets that are given protection may themselves escape attack.

Whilst a degree of displacement within specific categories of crime is to be expected, displacement from one form of crime to another seems less likely. The idea rests, to an extent, on the somewhat discredited view (cf. Clarke, 1977) that crime is committed by people with a propensity to criminal behaviour which will be expressed in one form or another whatever the hindrances and impediments. In fact, a great deal of crime is committed by people who would not ordinarily be thought of as 'criminal' and is heavily influenced by particular situational inducements and the balance of risks and rewards involved. Too little is known about these and it would seem that studies of the police effectiveness need to be complemented by further work concerned with the nature of crime and the psychological processes involved in a criminal act if the results are to be of practical assistance to the police in tailoring their activities to the facts of crime.

An alternative approach, discussed in Steenhuis' chapter does not so greatly encounter the problem of displacement in that it is intended to reduce peoples' inclinations to commit crimes of any sort. The innovations in Dutch policing which Steenhuis describes are closely identified with 'communal policing' or 'proactive policing', advocated most strongly in this country by John Alderson, Chief Constable of Devon and Cornwall Constabulary (Alderson, 1977). The primary form of prevention for which Steenhuis and Alderson argue comprises intervention intended to achieve a greater moral consensus: the police function is catalytic in producing this consensus, and involves strategies such as community liaison, schools liaison and youth work, as well as some of the more specific forms of intervention proposed by Engstad.

Communal policing, like the crime specific approach, is still very much an untested concept. The experience of the Devon and Cornwall Constabulary seems promising, but formal evaluations have still to be undertaken; the Dutch research which is in progress should provide much needed information. The extent to which it will reduce actual levels of crime remains to be seen; the track record of previous attempts at 'social' prevention is not encouraging. The approach holds out most promise in improving relations between the police and the (relatively) law abiding majority and in reducing fear of crime. For example a community project initiated by the National Association for the Care and Resettlement of Offenders, in which the police were quite heavily involved, was successful in improving morale on a problem estate, in reducing vandalism and in reducing fear of crime; but it is very unclear whether crimes other than vandalism were affected by the project (NACRO, 1978). Administrators may attach little importance to reductions in fear of crime; but Kelling (1978) has suggested that at least in the United States this fear has grown out of all proportion to the real danger, and that fear of crime is now a more serious social problem than crime itself.

Communal policing and the crime specific approach are clearly not mutually exclusive—simultaneous development seems both possible and desirable. However, they are likely to be subject to considerable resistance and scepticism, foremost from the police, and it would be rash to offer either as a panacea. Perhaps their best selling point is the absence of any well formulated alternatives for increasing the effectiveness of policing.

Note

This chapter carries Crown Copyright.

References

Alderson, J., (1977), *Communal Policing,* Devon and Cornwall Constabulary, Exeter.

Bittner, E., (1967), 'The police on skid-row', *American Sociological Review,* 5, pp. 699—715.

Boydstun, J. E., (1975), *San Diego Field Interrogation: Final Report,* Police Foundation, Washington, DC.

Bright, J. A., (1969), The Beat Patrol Experiment, Home Office Police Research and Development Branch, Report no. 7/69 (unpublished).

Cain, M., (1973), *Society and the Policeman's Role,* Routledge and Kegan Paul, London.

Chaiken, J. M., Lawless, M. W., and Stevenson, K. A., (1974), *The Impact of Police Activity on Subway Crime,* Rand Corporation, Santa Monica, Calif.

Chatterton, M., (1979), 'Police in social control', in Baldwin J., and Bottomley, A. K., (eds.), *Criminal Justice: Selected readings,* Martin Robertson, London.

Comrie, M. D., and Kings, E. J. (1975), 'Study of Urban Workloads: Final Report', Home Office Police Research Services Unit, (unpublished report).

Crust, P. E., (1975), 'Criminal Investigation Project', Home Office Police Research Services Unit (unpublished report).

Cumming E., Cumming I., and Edell, L., (1965), 'Policeman as philosopher, guide and friend', *Social Problems,* 12, pp. 276—86.

Clarke, R. V. G., (1977), 'Psychology and crime', *Bulletin of the British Psychological Society,* 30, pp. 280—3.

Clarke, R. V. G., (ed.) (1978), *Tackling Vandalism,* Home Office Research Study no. 47, HMSO, London.

Friedrich, R. J., (1979), 'The Impact of Organisational, Situational and Personal Factors on Police Behaviour', Michigan State University (unpublished dissertation).

Gates, D. F., and Knowles, L., (1976), 'An evaluation of the Rand Corporation's analysis of the criminal investigation process', *The Police Chief,* July.

Goldstein, H., (1977) *Policing a Free Society,* Ballinger, Cambridge, Mass.

Goldstein, J., (1960), 'Police discretion not to invoke the criminal process: low visibility decisions in the administration of justice', *Yale Law Journal,* 69, pp. 543—91.

Greenwood, P., Chaiken, J., and Petersilia, J., (1977) *The Criminal Investigation Process,* D. C. Heath, Lexington, Mass.

Halper, A., and Ku, R., (1975), *An Exemplary Project: New York City Police Department Street Crime Unit,* Law Enforcement

Assistance Administration, Washington, DC.

Heywood, R. (1979), 'Traditional and innovative policing', in Engstad, P., and Lioy, M., (eds.), *Proceedings: Workshop on Police Productivity and Performance*, Solicitor General of Canada, Ottawa, Ont.

Hough, J. M., (in preparation), 'Uniformed Police Work and Management Technology', Home Office Research Unit.

Holdaway, S., (1977), 'Changes in urban policing', *British Journal of Sociology*, 2, pp. 119—35.

Kansas City Police Department, (1978), *Response Time Analysis: Executive Summary*, Law Enforcement Assistance Administration, Washington, DC.

Kelling, G. L., Pate, T., Dieckman, D., and Brown, C. E., (1974), *The Kansas City Preventive Patrol Experiment: A Technical Report*, Police Foundation, Washington, DC.

Kelling, G. L., (1978), 'The quality of urban life and the police', in Conrad, J. D., (ed.) *The Evolution of Criminal Justice: A Guide for Practical Criminologists*, Sage Publications, Beverly Hills, Calif.

Larson, R. C., (1975), 'What happened to patrol operations in Kansas City? A review of the Kansas City Preventive Patrol Experiment', *Journal of Criminal Justice*, 3, pp. 267—97.

McCabe, M., and Sutcliffe, S., (1978), *Defining Crime: A study of police decision-making*, Blackwell, Oxford.

Manning, P., (1977), *Police Work: The Social Organisation of Policing*, MIT Press, London.

Martin, J. P., and Wilson, G., (1969), *The Police: A Study in Manpower,* Heinemann, London.

Mawby, R., (1979), *Policing the City*, Saxon House, Farnborough.

Mayhew, P., Clarke, R. V. G., Burrows, J. N., Hough, J. M., and Winchester, S. W. C., (1978), *Crime in Public View*, Home Office Research Study no. 49, HMSO, London.

National Association for the Care and Resettlement of Offenders (1978), *Cunningham Road Improvement Scheme: Impressions after Two Years*, London, NACRO.

New York Police Department (1955) *Operation 25.*

Pate, T., Bowers, R. A., and Parks, R., (1976), *Three Approaches to Criminal Apprehension in Kansas City: An Evaluation*, Police Foundation, Washington, DC.

President's Commission on Law Enforcement and the Administration of Justice (1967), *The Challenge of Crime in a Free Society*, U.S. Government Printing Office, Washington, DC.

Punch, M., (1979a), *Policing the Inner City*, Macmillan, London.

Punch, M., (1979b), 'A Mild Case of Police Corruption: Police Reactions in Amsterdam to Internal Deviance', unpublished paper delivered at the 1979 Annual Conference of the British Sociological Association.

Punch, M., and Naylor, T., (1973), 'The police: a social service', *New Society,* 17 May.

Reiss, A. J., (1971), *The Police and the Public,* Yale University Press, New Haven.

Reppetto T., (1974), *Residential Crime,* Ballinger, Cambridge, Mass.

Rubinstein, J., (1973), *City Police,* Farrar, Straus and Giroux, New York.

Schnelle, J. F., Kirchner, R. E., McNees, M. P., and Lawler, J. M., (1975) 'Social evaluation research: the evaluation of two police patrolling stragegies', *Journal of Applied Behaviour Analysis,* 4, pp. 353–65.

Schnelle, J. F., Kirchner, R. E. Casey, J. D., Useltor, P. H., and McNees, M. P., (1977), 'Patrol evaluation research: a multiple baseline analysis of police patrol during day and night hours', *Journal of Applied Behaviour Analysis,* 10, pp. 33–40.

Skolnick, J., (1966), *Justice Without Trial,* Wiley, New York.

Sparks, R. F., Genn, H. G., and Dodd, D. J., (1977), *Surveying Victims: A Study of the Measurement of Criminal Victimisation,* Wiley, Chichester.

Steer, D., (in preparation), 'The Police Role in Uncovering Crime', Police Staff College, Bramshill.

Wilson, J. Q., (1968), *Varieties of Police Behaviour,* Harvard University Press, Cambridge, Mass.

Woodley, A. C., (1976), Home Office Police Scientific Development Branch Research Note no. 8/76 (unpublished).

Zander, M., (1979), 'The investigation of crime: a study of cases tried at the Old Bailey', *Criminal Law Review,* April, pp.203–19.

2 Out of hugger-mugger: the case of police field services

David J. Farmer

The contemporary police institution—the complex of programmes, systems and job repertoires maintained by police management for 'determining' what officers do—remains less than adequate in meeting society's needs. Police research this decade has raised uncomfortable questions about this shortcoming and has suggested such avenues for improvement as a differential response strategy and purpose-oriented policing. By building on these foundations, social scientists and practitioners can reshape the nature and upgrade the calibre of police field services. But if they are to meet the needs of policing in the 1980s, police researchers must learn the lesson of the 1970s. These contentions are addressed in this paper in terms of experience gained from the considerable volume of research recently undertaken in the United States; in the past five years for instance, the National Institute of Law Enforcement and Criminal Justice (NILECJ) has developed and supported more than 75 major police research projects, representing an investment of more than $15 million. Some of these projects have been failures, requiring termination; some have evoked, in Wordsworth's phrase, 'the gloom of uninspired research', but an appreciable number compel attention from the police authorities. It is hoped the comments are relevant in other countries as they address the hugger-mugger (disorder, confusion, secrecy, muddle) in their police situations.

Research in the 1970s: the police—environment gap

To survive, an organisation must be both effective and efficient, as Chester Barnard (1938) points out. Effectiveness is defined as an appropriate relationship between the organisation and its environment; efficiency, a suitable relationship between an organisation and its members. Policing in the United States—and probably elsewhere—is hobbled on both these counts. Because police institutions are both public and necessary, they have escaped Barnardian extinction. But their survival in their present form has levied an unnecessary social cost: a lowering of the quality of life, particularly in the central city.

Obviously few, if any, organisations enjoy completely satisfactory external and internal relationships. Even so, it is contended that the primary problem of policing is the failure in the relationship between the police institution and its environment—and this is the focus of this section. Hamstrung by tradition and lack of understanding, the institutional practices of police do not adequately impact their environment. Intertwined is the related, but secondary, issue of the organisation's failure to relate suitably to its members. The problem as posed is essentially institutional, for the claim can be made that many individual police officers relate more effectively to their environments than do their agencies.

Nowhere is the police—environment gap clearer than in field services, such as patrol, criminal investigation and operational support.

Much of patrol is preventive—the conspicuous random movement of marked cars and uniformed personnel designed to create a feeling of 'police omnipresence' and thus to deter crime. Yet significant questions have been raised about the utility of preventive patrol, and the research raising these issues is discussed in Wilson (1975), Farmer (1976), O'Connor and Gilman (1978), and Chaiken (1978). For example a major experiment (Kelling et al., 1974) reported that variations in the level of the preventive patrol activity, within the staffing level of one American city, have a negligible effect on criminal activity and citizen satisfaction. Elsewhere, it is reported (Schnelle et al., 1977), that increases in night patrol coverage had an impact on the more serious (Part I) crime during a period of saturation patrol, but increases in the day patrols did not. Another study (Wilson and Boland, 1978) reports that police patrol strategies such as aggressive patrol affect the robbery rate.

The mixed messages that come from these and other studies (such as Press, 1971; Chaiken et al., 1975; as well as Bright, 1969) may be variously interpreted. One interpretation is that preventative patrol at the level and of the character usually undertaken in U.S. cities has negligible impact on the environment of crime and citizen satisfaction. Another is that, while some forms of preventative patrol are effective for some things, traditional preventive patrol is not effective in all respects. The cop on the corner might deter Toad of Toad Hall (a notorious hot-rodder) but not Willie Sutton (a notorious thief)—or, infractions on the street but not those in private places. Yet this might imply that traditional preventive patrol is an activity out of touch with its environment, and that police agencies can achieve an impact if they become more precise—like the surgeon—in their operations.

The major purposes of the criminal investigation process are solving cases and preparing evidence for the prosecutor. But one study reports that more than half of all serious reported crime receives only superficial attention from investigators, that an investigator's time is mainly taken up in work on cases that experience indicates will not be solved, and that prosecutors are hampered because investigators do not consistently and thoroughly document the key evidentiary facts (Greenwood et al., 1975). And other studies (e.g., Greenberg, 1976; Hayes, 1979) indicate that no systematic methods are used to apply investigative resources to cases according to their solvability prospects. Such studies imply that perhaps case clearance should no longer be considered the sole objective of detective work; how investigative activity could be made more responsive to society's needs should be the subject of further study.

Support services such as forensic science and crime analysis are key ingredients in effective operations. Yet even Sherlock Holmes would have been hard pressed had he relied on some of today's crime laboratories. A nationwide crime laboratory proficiency study reports many incorrect responses to test samples. Some of the higher levels of unacceptable responses were 67.8 per cent for hair-type, 21.5 per cent for wood, 71.2 per cent for blood, 28.2 per cent for firearms and 34 per cent for paint (Peterson, 1978). Crime analysis is a way by which police agencies can become institutionally aware of a significant segment of their work environment. Yet a lack of understanding and co-ordination between the analysts and the departments that use the analysis is reported (Reinier, 1977).

Additional evidence of the police-environment gap can be seen in the findings of the Kansas City Response Time Analysis Study (Bieck et al., 1977; in press). The results suggest the need to reconceptualise response time and question the principle (hitherto almost an article of faith in police operations) that agencies must be prepared to respond rapidly to all calls for service. Response time traditionally has been viewed as the time that elapses between the moment when the citizen calls and the point at which the police officer arrives at the scene. The time that elapses between the commission of the incident and the citizen's call which is frequently quite protracted has been ignored. Geared up to respond rapidly to all calls, police agencies have tried to act like an administrator who feels obliged to answer every telephone call whenever he receives it, regardless of whatever meetings or other commitments he may have, rather than returning calls as they fit in with the priorities of the working day.

Unlike earlier studies of police response time (e.g., Isaacs, 1967; Furstenberg, 1971; Clawson and Chang, 1975), the Kansas City study did not rely on officer self-reporting for data. Rather, it utilised civilian observers, the communications centre's tapes and interviews with victims and witnesses to analyse the relationship of police response time to arrests, evidence collection, injuries, officer safety and citizen satisfaction. A wealth of data was assembled on over 6,500 incidents, ranging from both serious and minor crime, to disturbances, reports of prowlers and suspicious persons, and general service calls. The study departs from the traditional view of response time as consisting of only communications and dispatch processing and police travel time to include the citizen mobilisation interval, which (in the best case, the median situation for Part I offences) comprises nearly half of the total response time continuum.

The study shows that rapid response is not necessary for the majority of police incidents. Concerning Part I (the more serious) offences, for example, Bieck (1977) writes that: 'First ... a large proportion of Part I crimes are not susceptible to the impact of rapid police response. Secondly, for that proportion of crimes that can be influenced by response time, the time taken to report the incident largely predetermines the effect of police response time'. At the same time, for a minority of calls such as crimes in progress rapid response is significant.

Bieck's recommendations demonstrate the gulf between the police agency and its environment:

1 'Procedures developed to discriminate accurately between emergency and non-emergency calls will achieve more productive outcomes if co-ordinated with patrol resource allocation'—not current practice.
2 'Because direct and rapid police response by non-dispatched officers to robbery incidents or to the immediate vicinity surrounding robbery scenes is not effective in achieving response related arrests, alternative response strategies for robberies should be developed, tested and evaluated'—not current practice.
3 'Because of the time citizens take to report crime, the application of technological innovations and human resources to reduce police response time will have negligible impact on crime outcomes'—not the accepted view.
4 And, finally, the 'realization which must be made is that rapid response is not a universal tactic, but rather a specific tool applicable only to certain types of incidents under specific circumstances'—not the current operating principle.

The extent of the police environment gap is also apparent in the various attempts being made to introduce field innovations. The technology varies, but as far as patrol is concerned, the organisational innovations fall into at least three major dimensions: the extent to which activities are directed, the extent of visibility and the extent of community orientation. Rather than the traditional approach of permitting officers to patrol at will in an assigned area, directed patrol involves the setting of particular patrol objectives—sometimes by the supervisor in consultation with the officer. This would include location-oriented patrol (where patrol officers concentrate on high crime areas) and crime specific patrols (where they concentrate on a specific type of offender); it would also refer to strategies such as split-force patrol where patrol strength is divided into a response, and a patrol, section. High visibility, a deterrence oriented activity, would include increased levels of traditional preventive patrol. Low visibility or plain clothes is directed towards arrests and employs blending and decoy techniques to intercept crimes. Community-oriented patrol, such as team policing, has the intention of identifying the police with a particular area and of decentralising decision-making. In the investigative area, the more significant innovations include methods of screening cases and of relating to patrol. While it would be unfair to characterise the foregoing as the efforts of police chiefs stumbling in the dark, the image has much to commend it.

A similar case could be made for a police-environment gap in the inter-organisational sphere—relations with the other public and private entities in the law enforcement industry, with social service agencies and with the rest of the criminal justice bureaucracies. To take the latter as an example, concern about transforming the criminal justice non-system into an integrated and smoothly functioning whole was voiced strongly by the 1967 President's Commission on Law Enforcement and Administration of Justice. The police still stand at the gateway of the criminal justice system, but the activities of other elements like parole remain of little concern to the gatekeeper. Traditional police organisations have not attempted to develop the administrative leadership and the organisational and procedural capability to relate effectively with these agencies. They probably will not do so until it is recognised that the 'community manager' concept should apply as much to the police chief as to the police officer.

A similar case could be made also for the internal relationships of the police agency—between the organisation and its members. These are marred by the undue autonomy of street personnel. As the literature on discretion and other aspects of policing implies, police agencies control the activities of street officers only within the broadest of limits (Goldstein, J., 1960; Piliavin and Briar, 1964; Wilson, 1968; Goldstein, H., 1970, 1977; Manning, 1978a). Thus, it is well known that 'police patrol officers exercise high levels of discretion, with the power to determine arrest without direction from their superiors', (Scott et al., 1977). Field units can operate with relative isolation from supervision and without effective monitoring by their bureaucracy. The extent of street level freedom from administrative

21

control in a paramilitary organisation reaches its most paradoxical in the failure of agencies to provide for effective anti-corruption management systems (Ward, 1979). That this control problem exceeds reasonable limits is clear when some departments do not know whether officers execute radio assignments and when some detectives investigate cases on the typewriter. The issue would be less troublesome if individual officers were faced with less temptations for malpractice and more incentives to perform effectively.

The general context of these failures of institutional relationships should be noted. There are almost 17,500 general purpose police agencies in the United States ranging in size from 30,000 to one person. Most have less than ten officers. In such a welter of agencies there is considerable variation in quality. The following would characterise (with important exceptions) aspects of the internal capability and style of medium sized and larger agencies:

1 Police chief: local person, risen through the ranks, minimal management training.
2 Other sworn personnel: local boys, multiple hierarchial levels, levels not well differentiated particularly in the middle.
3 Personnel system: informal, everybody knows everybody (big cities excepted), strong subculture code(s), paramilitary, civilians in clerical capacity only.
4 Planning function: grantsmanship, short term, limited skills.
5 Management style: management-by-crisis.
6 Operating principles: tradition, on your own, maintain control, cover yourself, get by.
7 Principal changes over past decade: more educated officers, more training, better equipment, more minority personnel, and more 'constitutional' procedures.

Within this context and with this capability (to the extent that this is realised in particular communities), the organisation must seek to establish effective external and efficient internal relationships.

And so on. The listing of operational issues and research is not intended to be comprehensive. Rather the purpose has been to illustrate the institutional inadequacy of the police function. To the extent that they succeed, police officers may well do so in spite of their organisations—like A-grade students and their teachers? The centrality of the police environment gap necessitates that police organisation remains a major focus of police research.

Narrowing the gap

The research discussed above promises to have a profound effect on

22

the structure of the police field survice delivery system in narrowing the gap between the police agency and its environment. Considered together, these studies have raised questions that suggest to some practitioners the desirability of reforming the entire system. The suggested direction is towards (a) more discrimination in addressing the needs of the environment, (b) adopting such techniques as a differential response system and (c) a purposive, rather than a process, orientation.

Every system, being embedded in other systems, operates under a number of constraints, both internal and external (Churchman, 1968). Examples of internal constraints are the available repertoire of standard operating procedures (see Allison, 1971) and existing staffing levels and capabilities. The external have been described (Manning, 1977) as relating to information, the law and citizen discretion. Such constraints limit the practitioner's opportunity to innovate, and s/he must usually employ strategies of 'disjointed incrementalism' (see Lindblom, 1959) or 'satisficing' rather than the strategies of optimisation advocated by 'scientific management'. For this reason, claims for the prospects of a research driven revolution in field service practice (Farmer, 1978a, b) perhaps should be reduced.

The kind of contribution that research might make to narrowing the police environment gap is perhaps best illustrated by describing some of the more recent NILECJ supported research aimed at developing methods of differential response to calls for assistance. A differential response differs from the present basis for handling calls for service. It does not treat each call as requiring (within the framework of a broad priority scheme) basically a similar response rendered as expeditiously as possible. Since the advent of the two-way radio and the automobile, this essentially undifferentiating response policy has typically involved the street bureaucrat in a pantomine of rapid automobile response, form-filling, coping and rapid return 'into service'—as if driving down the main road is a return to service. A differential response system would utilise a variety of responses: immediate with sirens and lights; delayed ('an officer will be there in thirty minutes'); appointments with an officer or civilian aide; telephone-reporting; walk-ins; and no response at all. It should be noted that some agencies have for a long time utilised some telephone reporting. A fully differentiated response system would require a fundamental administrative change in police agencies. It should not be dismissed as mere administrative tinkering because it can be used as a vehicle for meshing police agencies more responsively with their environment. And, in a bureaucracy, the structural and procedural change is the message.

Three NILECJ supported studies now in progress may provide

information concerning a differential police response system.

The citizen reporting component of the Kansas City Response Time Study is being replicated by the Police Executive Research Forum in four communities: San Diego, Peoria, Jacksonville-Duvall and Rochester. A report is anticipated next year. The intent is to determine the generalisability of the long victim and witness reporting times noted in Kansas City.

The City of Wilmington (Delaware) Police Department is attempting to examine the extent to which the demand for service can be modified, and the experience is being evaluated by Public Systems Evaluation. Wilmington's objective is a minimum reduction in call-for-service response workload of 20 per cent with a concomitant reduction in the responsive patrol force, while maintaining a ceiling on patrol car utilisation and critical call response time. Prior to the project, the City operated a 27 eight-hour car response force; this has been reduced to 21 eight-hour cars. These results were achieved through implementation of a complaint-screening system, providing referral, adjustment, walk-in, telephone and appointment response options. Larceny, malicious mischief and burglary offences have proved to be the most amenable to diversion from traditional response. Every non-critical complaint (where the crime is not in progress) in these categories is referred to a Complaint Service Unit. Most result in a phone report; alternatively a car responds by appointment. Thus, Tien (1978) reports that 'demand is being managed by elimination, internal response and scheduled external response'. And the nine-month programme has led to only two citizen complaints.

The City of Birmingham (Alabama) Police Department and the Police Executive Research Forum are studying 'Alternative Strategies for Responding to Calls for Service'. Information on the methods of mobilising the police is available from a number of earlier studies (e.g., Black, 1968; Bercal, 1970; Reiss, 1971; Meyer, 1976). Various methods of classifying calls have also been indicated (e.g., Cumming et al., 1965; Wilson, 1967; Reiss, 1971; Lilly, 1978). But these studies do not provide an operationally useful method of structuring a differential response system; the Birmingham study promises to do this. In addition, it has already collected evidence from sampling callers for police service in Birmingham and San Jose concerning citizen acceptance of deferred responses (Sumrall, in press). For example, slightly more than half the sample in the two cities expressed satisfaction with responses delayed up to 30 minutes, and a little under a half indicated satisfaction with the police making an appointment with the citizen.

Police agencies have programme purposes that are clear neither to police nor to others. Hence sociologists (e.g., Bittner, 1974) spend time considering what the purposes of policing may be. Hence NILECJ can support an ongoing study to examine these purposes. Meanwhile, most of police work is structured on a process, rather than a purposive, basis. Police agencies maintain units to undertake processes such as patrol and criminal investigation. The organisational and mental set is process: Dan O'Leary who walked his eight-hour tour, come rain or snow. Programme purpose is largely an alien afterthought.

A logical corollary of a field services delivery system restructured on a differential response basis would be a purposive programme designed to meet the needs of the work environment. In 1976, a minor by-product (Roscoe, 1976) of a large police study called Project STAR (Smith, 1976) was a projection of criminal justice needs during the balance of this century and suggestions concerning the changes in the police and criminal justice system required by these needs. These forecasts for the police serve to illustrate how police programmes could be constructed on a more purposive basis, with the purpose related to the work enviornment. Two examples taken from Roscoe (1976) are offered here. First, the 'organisational emphasis on efficiency and impersonal relationships characteristic of large police departments in urban regions diminishes the opportunities for personal face-to-face relationships between the police officer and the public and contributes to antagonistic police citizen interactions. Secondly, a 'large proportion of police officers who patrol the central cities of urban regions should be demilitarized and should be physically located full-time in urban schools, playgrounds, dance halls or other facilities frequented by young people. A major responsibility of these officers should be to establish and maintain communications links with young people'.

More focused policies, programmes, organisation and procedures, would help close the police environment gap, and the administrative and operating arrangements should be tailored to the policy and the programme. Problem-oriented policing (Goldstein, 1979) would be one approach to focusing policies and programmes. More appropriate use of command and control technology would facilitate this— intelligent technology driven by more realistic and human criteria than minimising response time and balancing workloads. Administrative structure also can be useful in this focusing. The Split Force Patrol approach was reported to have been helpful in giving impetus to the City of Wilmington Police Department, for example, in that it was claimed that a dedicated and directed patrol force could increase productivity: during the one year experiment (1975—76) increases were found in call-for-service response productivity, and in police professionalism and accountability (Tien, 1978). Other organisational mechanisms could be cited, including those facilitating interaction with private police and community capabilities. New procedures also could serve this purpose. Rather than relying on mere speed in direct response to major crime calls, for example, Bieck et al., (1977; in press) suggest that response alternatives could be developed that would improve arrest possibilities if information on the length of citizen reporting delays and criminal flight probabilities were built into agency procedures. Opportunities for this tactical management of field resources, co-ordinating resource disposition with communication procedures in terms of crime type and variations in citizen reporting delays, remain to be pursued seriously. Even forms can be designed to facilitate purposive action; the redesign of the preliminary investigation form by the City of Rochester is an example.

A realignment such as that described in the foregoing is suggested by the study of police matters. But the point should be underscored that police effectiveness, to the extent that it is built on scientific information, is not simply a function of studies of policing. Much that police do is not peculiar to policing, and knowledge and techniques available in a variety of sciences have been utilised directly in addressing police institutional and other problems. Psychology and forensic science provide examples. Research on subjects like motivation, for instance, has been used directly in police administration; the examples could be multiplied. More direct use of research results could be made. Standard police management textbooks (e.g., Wilson and McLaren, 1978), for example, do not reflect the fact that police management is a sub-topic of public administration, and an outstanding characteristic of police management literature is its intellectual insularity—its failure to incorporate what public administration can offer.

Research in the 1980s

The study of police matters—whether categorised as fundamental, practice-oriented or programmatic (Wirt, 1974)—has the objective of developing understanding of its principal environment, its subject matter. To achieve more effective understanding in coming years, police research (to continue the metaphor) should follow psycho-analytic practice and try to understand itself more fully. Poland's comment that evaluations frequently reveal more about social science than about the activity under evaluation deserves to be taken seriously. New initiatives are also needed in the substance of police studies.

Like a stick bent by refraction when poked into a stream, current social science methodologies applied to the covert environment of policing can give false impressions. This is partly a general problem of evaluation research—the difficulty referenced by Rossi when he writes (Rossi, 1978) that 'if there is any empirical law that is emerging from the past decade of widespread evaluation research activities, it is that the expected value for any measured effect of a social programme is zero', and that 'most programmes, when properly evaluated, turn out to be ineffective or at best marginally accomplishing their set aims'. But, partly, it stems from the nature of the police setting. While not unique to policing, the covert character does present acute problems—and this deserves emphasis.

Stated police purposes and procedures frequently differ from the actual ones, and police practitioners are often concerned to hide these realities. In their daily work, police commanders and officers frequently find it useful to employ deceit and bluff, and in their day-to-day activity the police officer feels above the minor provisions of the law. This is one reason why street officers are sometimes cynical about headquarters and the outside world; they know that they cannot and do not do their work according to the book. This has particular significance for data collection, analysis and evaluation—and it would be helpful in the coming years if students of police matters could benefit from the methodological experiences of the 1970s. (This is not intended to imply that police researchers devote no attention to their methods, e.g., Van Maanen, 1978.)

Such out-and-out wrongdoing as rigging data is, hopefully, foreign to most social scientists. But the difficulties in acquiring accurate data are severely compounded by the covert character of policing. A couple of illustrations will underscore this point. Operation 25, an experiment in manpower variation, was conducted in the New York City Police Department (N.Y.P.D., 1955) with a straight face and 'proved' the utility of additional police manpower. Although data manipulation claims have not been documented, it is clear that the data were rigged. The Chaiken (1975) study of subway crime in the same city suffered similarly, and the Transit Police Chief was investigated for encouraging data manipulation. As Chaiken reports, 'The authors of this study thought they observed a phenomenon in which criminals chose the hours before 8 p.m. and just after 4 a.m. to commit their crimes, knowing their risks of apprehension were lower than during the high patrol hours. Instead, the researchers were probably observing an artifact of data corruption' (Chaiken, 1978). Two other problems further compound the difficulty. First, most crime is not reported, and this characteristic of crime also facilitates the rigging of research data. Second, many social scientists are inclined to believe data, particularly if they are in official records. It is difficult for them to penetrate the mental veil into police work, where false reporting, misrepresentation and manipulation are parts of the work life. At the beginning of every shift in New York City in the early 1970s, for example, each precinct reported its manpower disposition to the Command and Control Center where the data were tabulated by computer; yet the figures were recognised at headquarters as false. The examples could be multiplied (e.g., Manning, 1978), and it is observed that 'deceit, evasiveness, duplicity, lying, innuendo, secrecy, double-talk and triple-talk mark many of the interactions in police agencies', (Van Maanen, 1978). Those who do not understand the pervasiveness of misrepresentation in police life fail to understand policing.

The police researcher in the coming years will surely be more conscious of this methodological reality. S/he will surely abandon mail questionnaire surveys, a problem exacerbated by the volume of such surveys and the tendency of police chiefs to have them answered by someone like a patrol officer in the Planning Division. S/he will surely anticipate sophisticated attempts to subvert experiments and adopt correspondingly sophisticated controls. Even Automated Vehicle Monitoring can be frustrated, for example, as the St Louis experience suggests. S/he will surely adopt a 'false until proven true' attitude toward police records. S/he will surely involve police practitioners more routinely in data analysis and evaluation in order to catch the obvious frauds.

Data collection and analysis in the 1980s can be expected to improve. It is hoped that experimentation will become more commonplace and not confined to exceptions like the Kansas City Preventive Patrol and the Seattle Hidden Camera experiments, (Whitcomb, 1979). Experiments are significant because, unlike one-shot case studies, they provide higher levels of confidence. Experiments set the treatment and control groups apart prior to measurement, examine 'before' and 'after' measures to identify effects as well as differences between the two groups, and attempt to establish controls in the police setting, similar to those effected in the laboratory. It is also hoped that data sharing will occur more frequently, permitting not only substantial economies of effort but also secondary analyses. To mention only two, masses of sound data exist in the Kansas City Police Department and the Workshop in Political Theory and Policy Analysis at Bloomington; they should be used to the fullest.

Analysis in the 1980s also could improve if criticisms were accepted more readily, if researchers were more accountable in laying open their data bases for outside inspection, and if studies were not accepted so readily on their face value. A fledgeling subject perhaps has greater need for defensiveness; hopefully, this need will decline in the coming years. Analysis may also improve through greater use of cross-national studies. Such studies can have the advantage of identifying police activities that are arbitrary and culturally determined, thus suggesting opportunities for improvements. But, beyond this, they help to counteract the parochial approach that is marked in addressing police issues today, as can be seen in the example of American police management literature mentioned earlier.

Substance

Police institutional inadequacy, the police–environment gap, should remain a central concern of practice oriented police research for a number of years. This statement attests to the crucial character of the institutional problem for police performance. It also reflects the fact that institutional adjustment is the readiest method for effecting change. But it does not deny the importance of analysing methods for removing the appendix (i.e., 'real' police work), as compared with hospital administration (i.e., mere administration), to use Bittner's analogy. Surely, concern with the 'craft of policing'—with developing effective and professional operating procedures and techniques at the individual police officer level—should be a major additional research emphasis during the eighties.

NILECJ, the principal source of support for police research in the United States, presently intends to retain research on improvements in the police field services system (expressed as 'the allocation and deployment of police resources') as its principal police research priority. For this purpose, it seeks to support research that will develop additional insights into the objectives of policing, into current operations, and into alternative approaches for providing field services. What should be the objectives of police operations? How effective are current police operations? What are the alternative approaches for providing field services?

With this in mind, NILECJ projects being initiated this year include an experiment to replicate the intent of the Kansas City preventive patrol project; further examination of investigative behaviour, preferably on a cross-national basis; study of the police use of deadly force; research on the implications of crime-focused policing; and analysis of the utilisation of forensic science in police investigations. During the coming year, projects are planned to analyse the learning sources for police job repertoires, the relationship of policing with interest groups, the variations in the factors that trigger a citizen to

29

call for police services, the implications of utilising a problem-focused approach to policing, the relevance of future study to police problems and the relationship of public and private policing. To further its objectives, NILECJ is also supporting research to synthesise and analyse the results of research. Last year such a project was initiated to synthesise research on police operations; this year will see a synthesis started on police management. The intention is in future years to undertake additional synthesis projects on other sub-topics, other perspectives. The likelihood is that the National Institute of Justice (NIJ), which Congress is considering creating as a replacement for NILECJ, will retain the present direction of police research activity. However, the reorganisation does introduce additional uncertainty, and supplementary emphasis (such as concern for developing the craft of policing) is likely. These efforts will affect the character of the study of police matters and, hopefully, the police environment gap.

Beyond this, Alice Rivlin's (1971) prescription concerning systematic thinking for social action seems apt for future research intended to strengthen the police institution. The police and the public need to know what works and how to provide better services in a changing environment. Systematic experimentation—designing programmes in varying ways with the deliberate intention of building a body of knowledge about what works—would be ideal. While reliance in our society may well remain on random and natural experimentation, systematic experimentation should not be viewed as an impossible dream. Of course, such evaluative research is linked with two basic needs; better understanding of the functions and activities of policing and more capability for measuring. Some progress has been made in understanding policing, but widespread contempt for research on the part of practitioners hints at the gulf that still exists. Limited progress (e.g., Needle, 1979), also has been made in working toward the development of police programme performance measurement system(s), but achieving the goal remains far off. Police research in the seventies has demonstrated the utility of studying police matters. Needed in the eighties are improvements on this experience, along the lines discussed here, if the character of policing and of society is not to deteriorate.

Notes

The author is currently director of the Police Division in the National Institute of Law Enforcement and Criminal Justice. However the points of view or opinions in this chapter are those of the author and do not necessarily represent the official position or policies of the US Department of Justice, LEAA, or NILECJ.

References

Allison, G. T., (1971), *Essence of Decision: Explaining the Cuban Missile Crisis,* Little, Brown and Company, Boston, Mass.

Bercal, T. E., (1970), 'Calls for police', *American Behavioural Scientist,* 13, pp. 681—91.

Barnard, C., (1938), *The Functions of the Executive,* Harvard University Press, Cambridge, Mass.

Black, D. J., (1968), *Police Encounters and Social Organisation: An Observational Study,* Ann Arbor, Mich.

Bieck, W., et al., (1977), *Response Time Analysis, (Summary, Vol. I Methodology, Vol. II Analysis,* Kansas City Police Department, Kansas City, Mo.

Bieck, W., et al., (in press), *Response Time Analysis, (Vol. III Part II Crime Analysis, Vol. IV Non Crime Calls Analysis, Vol. V Prosecutorial Follow-Up Analysis,* Kansas City Police Department, Kansas City, Mo.

Bittner, E., (1974), 'Florence Nightingale in pursuit of Willie Sutton: a theory of the police', in Jacob H., (ed.), *The Potential for Reform of Criminal Justice,* Sage Publications, Beverly Hills, Calif.

Bright, J. A., (1969), *Beat Patrol Experiment,* Home Office, London.

Chaiken, J. M., Lawless, M. W., and Stevenson, K. A., (1975), *The Impact of Police Activity on Crime Robberies in the New York City Subway System,* Rand Corporation, Santa Monica, Calif.

Chaiken, J. M., (1978), 'What is known about the deterrent effects of police activities', in Cramer, J. A., (ed.), *Preventing Crime,* Sage Publications, Beverly Hills, Calif.

Churchman, C. W., (1968), *The Systems Approach,* Dell Publishing Co., New York.

Clawson, C., and Chang, C., (1975), *Impact of Response Delays on Arrest Rates* and *Analysis of the Patrol-Dispatch Operation,* unpublished report, Seattle Police Department, Seattle, Wash.

Cumming, E., Cumming, I., and Edell, L., (1965), 'Policeman as philosopher, guide and friend', *Social Problems,* 12, pp. 276—86.

Farmer, D. J., (1976), 'Fact versus fact: a selective view of police research in the United States', *The Police Journal,* 49, pp. 104—13.

Farmer, D. J., (1978a), 'The future of local law enforcement in the United States: the Federal role', *Police Studies,* 1, pp. 31—8.

Farmer, D. J., (1978b), 'The research revolution', *Police Magazine,* 4, pp. 64—5.

Furstenberg, F. F., (1971), *Strategies of Evaluating Police Performance*, American Society of Criminology, unpublished.

Goldstein, H., (1970), 'Police response to urban crisis', in Summers, M., and Barth, T., (eds.), *Law and Order in a Democratic Society*, pp. 143—53, Charles E. Merrill, Columbus, Ohio.

Goldstein, H., (1977), 'Policing: a problem oriented approach', *Crime and Delinquency*, 1, pp. 237—58.

Goldstein, J., (1960), 'Police discretion not to invoke the criminal process: low visibility decisions in the administration of justice', *Yale Law Review*, 69, pp. 543—94.

Greenberg, B., (1976), *Felony Investigation Decision Model: an Analysis of Investigative Elements of Information*, Stanford Research Institute, Menlo Park, Calif.

Greenwood, P. W., Chaiken, J. M., Petersilia, J., and Prusoff, L., (1975), *The Criminal Investigation Process*, Rand Corporation, Santa Monica, Calif.

Hayes, G., (in press), *Alternative Strategies for Responding to Calls for Service*, Police Executive Research Forum, Washington, DC.

Hayes, G., (in press), *Manual for Conducting the Burglary Investigation Decision Model Replication (BIDMOR)*, Police Executive Research Forum, Washington, DC.

Isaacs, H. H., (1967), 'A study of communications, crimes and arrests in a Metropolitan police department', *Task Force Report: Science and Technology*, pp. 88—106, US Government Printing Office, Washington, DC.

Kelling, G. L., Pate, T., Dieckman, D., and Brown, C. E., (1974), *The Kansas City Preventive Patrol Experiment: A Technical Report*, Police Foundation, Washington, DC.

Lilly, R. J., (1978), 'What are the police now doing?' *Journal of Police Science and Administration*, 6, p. 51.

Lindblom, C. E., (1959), 'The science of muddling through', *Public Adminstration Review*, 19, pp. 79—88.

O'Connor, R. J., and Gilman, B., (1978), 'The police role in deterring crime', in Cramer, J. A., (ed.), *Preventing Crime*, Sage Publications, Beverly Hills, Calif.

Manning, P., (1977), *Police Work: The Social Organization of Policing*, Massachusetts Institute of Technology Press, Cambridge, Mass.

Manning, P., (1978a), *Police Narcotics Control: Patterns and Strategies*, US Government Printing Office, Washington, DC.

Manning, P., (1978b), 'Foreword', in Wickman, P., and Whitten, P., (eds.), *Readings in Criminology*, D. C. Heath, Lexington, Mass.

Manning, P., (1978c), 'Lying, secrecy and social control', in Manning, P., and Van Maanen, J., (eds.), *Policing: A View from the Street*,

Goodyear, Santa Monica, Calif.

Meyer, C., (1974), 'Patterns of reporting noncriminal incidents to the police', *Criminology,* 12, pp. 70—83.

Needle, J., (in press), *Police Programme Performance Measurement,* American Justice Institute, Sacramento, Calif.

New York Police Department (1955), 'Operation 25'.

Peterson, J., (1978), *Crime Laboratory Proficiency Study,* US Government Printing Office, Washington, DC.

Piliavin, I., and Briar, S., (1964), 'Police encounters with juveniles', *American Journal of Sociology,* 70, pp. 206—14.

Press, S. J., (1971), *Some Effects of an Increase in Police Manpower in the 20th Precinct of New York City,* Rand Institute, New York.

Reinier, G. H., (1977), *Crime Analysis,* US Government Printing Office, Washington, DC.

Reiss, A. J., (1971), *The Police and the Public,* Yale University Press, New Haven, Conn.

Rivlin, A., (1971), *Systematic Thinking for Social Action,* The Brookings Institution, Washington, DC.

Roscoe, P., (1976), *The Impact of Social Trends on Crime and Criminal Justice,* Anderson-Davis, Cincinnati, Ohio.

Schnelle, J. F., Kirchner, R. E., McNees, M. P., and Lawler, J. M., (1977), 'Patrol evaluation research: a multiple-baseline analysis of saturation police patrolling during day and night hours', *Journal of Applied Behaviour Analysis,* 10, pp. 33—40.

Scott, E. J., (1977), *Case Disposition: An Assessment of Literature on Police Referral Practices,* Workshop in Political Theory and Police Analysis, Bloomington, Indiana.

Smith, C. P., (1976), *Role Performance and the Criminal Justice System,* Anderson-Davis, Cincinnati, Ohio.

Sumrall, R., (in press), *Alternative Strategies for Responding to Police Calls for Services,* Birmingham Police Department, Birmingham, Alabama.

Tien, J., (1978), *An Evaluation Report of an Alternative Approach in Police Patrol: the Wilmington Split Force Experiment,* US Government Printing Office, Washington, DC.

Van Maanen, J., (1978), 'Epilogue: on watching the watchers', in Manning, P., and Van Maanen, J., (eds.), *Policing: A View from the Street,* Goodyear, Santa Monica, Calif.

Ward, R., and McCormack, R., (1979), *An Anti-Corruption Manual for Administrators in Law Enforcement,* John Jay Press, New York.

Whitcomb, D., (1979), *Focus on Robbery: the Seattle Hidden Camera Project,* US Government Printing Office, Washington, DC.

Wilson, J. Q., and Boland, B., (1978), 'The effect of the police on crime', *Law and Society Review,* 12, pp. 367—90.

Wilson, J. Q., (1975), *Thinking about Crime*, Basic Books, New York.

Wilson, O. W., and McLaren, R., (1978), *Police Administration*, (first edition, 1950), McGraw-Hill, New York.

Wirt, J. G., and Lieberman, A. J., (1974), *R and D Management: Methods Used by Federal Agencies*, The Rand Corporation, Santa Monica, Calif.

3 The Rand study of criminal investigation: the findings and its impact to date

Peter W. Greenwood

Introduction

In 1973 The Rand Corporation was awarded a grant by the National Institute of Law Enforcement and Criminal Justice (NILECJ) to undertake a nationwide study of the criminal investigation practices of major metropolitan police agencies (Greenwood et al., 1977). The purposes of the study were to describe how police investigations were organised and managed and to assess the contribution of various investigation activities to overall police effectiveness. Prior to the Rand study, police investigators had not been subject to the type of analytic scrutiny which was being focused on other types of police activity. Most police administrators knew little about the effectiveness or day-to-day activities of their investigative units and even less about the practices of other departments. The purpose of this paper is to summarise the findings from the Rand study, which the author directed, and to describe some of the impacts which the study has had.

The study design

The Rand study concentrated on the investigation of index offences—serious crimes against unwilling victims, as opposed to vice, narcotics, gambling or traffic offences. Information on current practices was obtained by a national survey of all municipal or county police agencies that employed more than 150 officers or that served jurisdictions with a 1970 population in excess of 100,000. Interviews and observations were conducted in more than 25 departments selected to represent different investigative styles. Data on investigation outcomes were obtained from the Uniform Crime Report (UCR) tapes maintained by the FBI; samples of completed cases, which were coded for the purpose of this study; and internal evaluations or statistics compiled by individual departments. Data on the allocation of investigation efforts were obtained from a computerised workload file maintained by the Kansas City Police Department.

The national survey and UCR data were combined for the purposes of analysing relationships between departmental characteristics and apprehension effectiveness. The special case samples were analysed to determine how specific cases were actually solved.

Investigative efforts and arrests

One of the principal problems confronted in evaluating investigative units lies in determining how their effectiveness is to be measured. A number of earlier studies conducted in individual cities suggested that clearance rates were an inappropriate measure of police performance—a finding which was confirmed by the Rand study. Our own analysis of 1972 UCR data showed that the number of clearances claimed for each index arrest ranged from a low of 0.38 to a high of 4.04 among the departments we studied. These differences appeared to be related to differences in definition and administrative practice rather than any real differences in investigative outcomes.

Even arrest rates appear to be too gross a measure to reflect the contribution of investigative units. The Rand study disclosed that approximately 30 per cent of all index arrests were produced by patrol officers responding to the scene of a crime. In roughly another 50 per cent of all index arrests, the identity of the perpetrator was supplied by a victim or witness at the time of the initial crime report, leaving only about 20 per cent of arrests which could possibly be attributed to the efforts of investigative units.

But even in this 20 per cent of initially unsolved cases, we found that investigators did not play a predominant role. Most of them were eventually solved by subsequent patrol arrests, spontaneous information provided by members of the general public (as opposed to informants) or routine clerical actions such as the checking of licence plates. Only about 3 per cent of all index arrests appeared to result from special investigative efforts where organisation, training or skill could make any conceivable difference.

This finding was confirmed by our analysis of differences among departments in their individual arrest rates. The number of reported offences resulting in an arrest was inversely related to a department's workload but not to its method of organisation. Departments with higher numbers of reported crimes per sworn officer report lower rates of arrest. However, differences in the allocation of manpower between uniformed patrol and investigators, or different methods of organising investigative functions did not result in different arrest rates.

How an investigator's time is spent

Whether or not a department uses any type of formal screening system to weed out unsolvable cases, our survey disclosed that most property offences receive only cursory attention. Although an investigator may carry a backlog of several hundred cases, only a small percentage are realistically considered active.

The Rand study revealed that an investigator's time on casework is predominantly consumed in reviewing reports, documenting files, and attempting to locate and interview victims. In cases that are eventually solved, he spends more time in post-arrest processing than he does in apprehending the suspect. Almost half of a typical investigator's time is devoted to such activities as administrative assignments or general surveillance which are not directly related to casework and are unlikely to produce arrests.

We did not find much attention devoted to investigator training or management. Most departments do not offer any special training when an officer is promoted from patrol to investigations. Investigative skills are expected to be acquired on the job. Supervisors of investigative units do not ordinarily review or even remain aware of the day-to-day performance of their men. Their attention is normally devoted to more routine personnel matters or dealing with an occasional very hot case.

The collection and processing of physical evidence

Our survey disclosed that many departments had begun using special technicians to collect physical evidence—primarily fingerprints and photographs from crime scenes. From an analysis of six departments which utilised different evidence collection procedures, we established that the amount and quality of evidence obtained was positively related to the amount of effort devoted to crime scene search and the speed with which technicians were dispatched.

However, the percentage of case solutions resulting from latent print identifications was unrelated to the print recovery rate. The reason for this somewhat surprising finding appeared to be that most police departments did not have adequate resources devoted to their latent search capability. They were unable to utilise those prints that were lifted. In most departments, latent prints were only utilised to confirm the identity of a suspect which had been established in some other way. 'Cold searches' of latent prints against 'known offender' files were rarely attempted, although some departments had demonstrated that they can be quite productive.

Preparing a case for prosecution

In general, we found police investigators more oriented toward clearing cases, rather than the problems of successful prosecution following an arrest. The inability to convict a defendant was looked on as a problem for the prosecutor and the courts rather than a matter over which the police could exercise much control.

Subsequent to the Rand study, a number of researchers have shown that less than half of all felony arrests result in successful prosecution. The predominant reason for this high case drop out rate appears to be witness co-operation. Research has also established that efforts by the police to obtain corroborating physical evidence or the testimony of more than one witness results in higher conviction rates (Forst, 1978).

The Rand study examined the relationship between investigation thoroughness and conviction rates by comparing two jurisdictions which differed significantly in the quality of information contained in their investigation reports. Using a checklist of 39 evidentiary questions which might be pertinent to a robbery prosecution, the more thorough jurisdiction averaged 45 per cent coverage of these items while the less thorough jurisdiction averaged only 26 per cent coverage. As a result, the more thorough jurisdiction was able to achieve a much higher conviction rate and much greater likelihood of conviction on the original charge.

Other findings

One of the frequent rationalisations which is offered for the policy of routinely assigning an investigator to all offences is that the public demands it. Administrators express a reluctance to close unsolvable cases without some token efforts by an investigator to keep the victim happy. A small victim survey conducted in one jurisdiction, as part of the Rand study, disclosed that this concern on the part of police management was not justified. Most victims would appear to accept the police department's decision to suspend their case without any great resentment. Nevertheless, most say they would appreciate being informed if a suspect is eventually caught, regardless of whether the offender is ever charged with their particular crime or their property is returned.

Policy recommendations

Based on our research findings, we offered a number of policy suggestions which might increase a police department's investigation effectiveness by either reducing resources, increasing apprehension rates or both.

First, we suggested that post-arrest investigation activities be co-ordinated more directly with the prosecutor by either assigning investigators to his office or by allowing him to exert more guidance over the policies and practices which they follow. This move was expected to result in a higher percentage of prosecutable cases.

Secondly, we suggested that patrol officers be given a larger role in conducting preliminary investigations, both to provide an adequate basis for case screening and to eliminate the need for redundant efforts by an investigator. It appears that most cases can be closed on the basis of the preliminary investigation and that patrol officers can be trained to conduct them adequately. This expanded role for patrol officers is also consistent with other moves toward geographic decentralisation and patrol officer job enrichment.

We also recommended that additional resources be devoted to processing latent prints and that improved systems be developed for organising and searching latent print files.

Finally, in conducting follow-up investigations for those cases which a department elected to pursue, we recommended that they distinguish between those cases which involved only routine clerical processing and those involving special investigation or legal skills. The former could be handled by lower level clerical personnel while the latter could be assigned to a major offence bureau for careful monitoring and continuous evaluation.

Impact of the findings

Following its release, the Rand study was given extremely wide coverage in the popular media and was the subject of heated controversy within the police profession. Many police officials, especially those who had not come up through the detective ranks, were sympathetic to the study in that it supported their own impressions of how investigators functioned. Some went so far as to criticise the report for 'telling us what we already knew'. A number of police chiefs were hostile to the report because it was being used by other city officials as an excuse to cut police budgets. Others refused to accept the findings because of the limited number of departments from which some of the principal findings were drawn, (cf. NILECJ, 1977).

Although there have not been any major attempts to replicate or extend the findings of the Rand study, there have been several reports published which contain findings that are consistent with our own. Bloch and Weidman's (1976) analysis of the Rochester, New York police department's investigation practices and Greenburg's (1977) efforts to develop a felony investigation decision model both resulted in findings supportive of the notion that the preliminary investigation conducted by patrol officers produce the majority of arrests and can provide adequate information for screening out unsolvable cases. A report by the Vera Institute (1977) on felony arrest dispositions in New York City supplied evidence that a substantial portion of felony arrests for street crimes involve offenders who are known to their victims. A report by Brian Forst (1978) on the disposition of Washington DC felony arrests demonstrates the importance of physical evidence and multiple witnesses in securing convictions for felony street crimes.

Following up on the interest in investigation policy, which was generated by the Rand study, NILECJ sponsored a series of regional workshops to assist police administrators in assessing the reforms which had been suggested and planning for their implementation. These workshops were developed and run by the University Research Corporation and drew heavily on the materials contained in the Rand, Bloch and Greenberg studies.[1] These workshops were extremely well received by the police officials who attended them with a majority reporting that they intended to implement policy changes they had developed as a result of attending the workshop.

In an additional effort to demonstrate the practical value of recent research on investigation practices, NILECJ awarded grants to five police departments[2] which had indicated an interest in implementing a number of investigative reforms. Although the demonstration was to have been evaluated by an outside contractor, it was not conceived as an experimental test of any particular reforms. Rather, its purpose was to determine how police departments would go about implementing reforms when they were given the freedom and resources to do so.

The participating departments were encouraged to concentrate on reforms in the following five areas:

1 *Initial investigations.* Patrol officers were to be given greater responsibility for initial investigations with their attention focused on the presence or absence of specific 'solvability factors' which would determine whether a case should be continued or closed.
2 *Case screening.* A formal system of case screening was to be developed to select cases which merited continuation, based on the information disclosed by the patrol officer's initial investigation.
3 *Managing the continuing investigation.* Investigation supervisors were to develop techniques for the systematic assignment of cases

40

and periodic review of their progress.

4 *Police-prosecutor relations.* The degree of co-ordination between police investigation and prosecution activities was to be expanded with the objective of increasing the percentage of cases accepted for prosecution.

5 *Investigation monitoring system.* Each department was to develop a statistical reporting system which could be used to evaluate the effectiveness of specific investigative units.

Unfortunately, the experiences of the five demonstration sites do not provide an adequate basis for determining the value of any particular reforms, due to major programme differences between sites and the failure of the national evaluator to produce a final report. Nevertheless, a limited number of lessons can be drawn from the demonstration, based on interviews with the participants and observations by outside observers:[3]

1 Those departments which substantially expanded the patrol officer's role in conducting initial investigations experienced a significant increase in the time required for these investigations to be conducted.

2 Regardless of the criteria which were formally specified for case closure decisions, case screening appeared to be highly subjective in most departments.

3 Although case screening resulted in substantially lower investigator caseloads, only one department elected to make any substantial reduction in its number of investigators.

4 None of the departments met with any significant community dissatisfaction as a result of instituting a policy of early case closure without investigator follow up. All of them adopted some form of written notification to inform victims of the status of their case.

5 The two departments which worked with their prosecutors to improve the quality of their cases, and kept records of the results, reported a significant increase in the percentage of cases accepted for prosecution.

6 None of the departments developed a statistical reporting system which was adequate for evaluative purposes.

7 None of the departments reported a significant change in arrest or clearance rates which could be attributed to changes in their investigation practices.

In addition to whatever reforms were prompted by the workshops and demonstrations programmes, a number of departments have instigated investigative reforms under other LEAA programmes.[4] The Career Criminal Program, which focuses prosecution resources on locally identified career criminals, has resulted in much closer working relationships between police investigators and deputy prosecutors in many of the participating jurisdictions, (Dahman and Lacy, 1977). Departments participating in the Integrated Criminal Apprehension Program (ICAP) have been encouraged to improve the quality of their patrol officers' preliminary investigations and to focus the efforts of their investigators on series of crimes which can be identified by statistically analysing the patterns of reported incidents, (LEAA, 1978). No specific results from these programmes have been reported to date.

In summary, recent research on criminal investigation practices, and the demonstration projects it has prompted, tells us more about what does not work than what does. The Rand study demonstrated that investigative activities play only a minor role in contributing to overall arrest rates, and that much of an investigator's time is consumed with administrative paperwork or attempting to locate and interview witnesses on cases that empirical evidence show have a small likelihood of ever being solved. Although the Rand study and other researchers have suggested a number of innovations which could conceivably improve the performance of investigative units, the effectiveness of these reforms has not been demonstrated to date.

Notes

1 See Cawley and Myron (1975) for the text which was used in these workshops.
2 Rochester, New York; Montgomery County, Maryland; Birmingham, Alabama; Santa Monica, California; and St Paul, Minnesota.
3 In addition to my own conversations with project staff, I have had the opportunity to review a draft programme designed by Ilene Greenberg and Robert Wasserman of ABT Associates who visited each of the project sites.
4 The workshops and five-site demonstration programme were both called 'Managing Criminal Investigations'.

References

Bloch, P., and Bell, J., (1976), *Managing Investigations: The Rochester System,* Police Foundation, Washington, DC.
Bloch, P., and Weidman, D., (1975), *Managing Criminal Investigations: Prescriptive Package,* US Government Printing Office, Washington, DC.

Cawley, D., and Miron, H., (1977), *Managing Criminal Investigations: Manual,* University Research Corporation, Washington, DC.

Dahman, J., and Lacy, J., (1977), *Criminal Prosecution in Four Jurisdictions: Departures from Routine Processing in the Career Criminal Program,* Metrek Division of the Mitre Corporation, McLean, Va.

Forst, B., (1978), *What Happens After Arrest,* US Government Printing Office, Washington, DC.

Greenberg, B., (1977), *Felony Investigation Decision Model: An Analysis of Investigative Elements of Information,* US Government Printing Office, Washington, DC.

Greenwood, P., (1970), *An Analysis of the Apprehension Activities of the New York City Police Department,* The New York City—Rand Institute, R-529-NYC.

Greenwood, P., Chaiken, J., and Petersilia, J., (1977), *The Criminal Investigation Process,* D. C. Heath, Lexington, Mass.

Johnston, H., (1979), *Managing Criminal Investigations in Santa Monica, California: A Case Study,* The Urban Institute, Washington, DC.

Law Enforcement Assistance Administration, (1978), *Integrated Criminal Apprehension Program. Review of Patrol Operations Analysis: Selected Readings from ICAP Cities,* US Department of Justice, Washington, DC.

National Institute of Law Enforcement and Criminal Justice, (1977), *The Criminal Investigation Process: A Dialogue on Research Findings,* US Government Printing Office, Washington, DC.

4 Policing: a research agenda for rational policy making

George L. Kelling, Mary Ann Wycoff and Tony Pate
(with the assistance of Charles Susmilch and Charles Brown)

The primary purpose of research into policing is to provide understandings which will lead to basic improvements in how quality
police services are provided. It is for that reason that this paper will
try to analyse the extent to which existent research is relevant to
policy development. The research agenda which we will propose has
that practical purpose in mind.

It is possible to take polar positions on the state of current research into policing in the United States. On the one hand, it can
be argued that we are into the second and third generation of police
research, that some of the research into policing has been at a high
level of methodological sophistication, and that we now are at a
point where major synthesising efforts are appropriate. One of the
authors of this paper has published several articles taking this point
of view (Kelling and Fogel, 1978, Kelling 1978). Another of the
authors, however, has taken the exact opposite point of view: that
research into policing has been fragmentary; has neither built on its
strengths nor learned from its mistakes; has not been based on an
overall conceptual scheme that identifies the important research
areas; and has only skimmed, in the most cursory way, over many
of the most critical areas. This point of view argues that what is
needed is not a synthesis of what we know, but rather a synthesis
or conceptual framework of what we do *not* know so that a research
agenda can be developed. This paper will attempt to develop such an
overview. We will discuss four broad areas: the demand for police
service; the type or quality of service delivered; the capacity to respond to the demand; and the outcomes of police service.

These are not just academic issues. They are central to the development of rational policy. Because many of these issues have only
been dealt with superficially, police have difficulty in: selecting
personnel rationally; training personnel adequately; deploying personnel rationally; rewarding quality performance; defining appropriate
levels or quality of education for police; differentially responding to
calls for service; planning service; doing cost benefit analyses of their
services; and measuring organisational success.

In discussing a research agenda with which to identify what we have learned and, equally important, what we have not learned, we will borrow some of the language of role theory. All of the knowledge we would deem critical to the rational development of policy can be conceptualised in role terms. The demand for service is a major determinant of *role content,* the job that police are asked to do. *Role enactment* is the way in which police respond to that demand. Organisationally, it refers to the types and numbers of services delivered and the way in which they are delivered. For the individual officer, it refers to the manner in which the assigned job is handled. *Role capacity* refers to the technology, strategies and human skills with which the organisation produces its role enactment. The consequences of the way in which the capacity is used to create the performance can be thought of as *role outcomes.*

Role content

Quite a bit of research has been done to identify those jobs which police are expected to do. This work includes analysis of calls for service (Cumming, et al., 1965; Bercal, 1970; Ostrom, 1979; Bieck, 1977a; and others), job and task analyses (California Commission, 1978; Rosenfeld and Thornton, 1976; Goodgame and Rao; Houston Police Department, 1976; Wollack and Associates, and others), and studies of citizen and officer expectations (e.g., Police Foundation Kansas City Citizen Survey, 1972; Police Foundation Survey of Robbery Victims and Witnesses, 1977; Newark Survey of Public Attitudes (Guyot, 1977), and several surveys of police officers).

While this type of research is critical to understanding what it is police currently are expected to do in our society, it is inadequate for understanding what changing and future expectations of the police are likely to be. While role content research has been useful for helping police understand where they are, there is nothing in it which suggests where they ought to be or how they ought to perform. It provides no basis for planning, recruitment, training, or strategy or budgeting policy which will meet future demands for service.

If police are to be able to plan for the future rather than only respond to present emergencies, we would argue that an understanding of role content must be supported by knowledge about the *source* of the demands or requests for police service. Demands for police service are of at least three types:

1 *Spontaneous requests* for service in response to specific incidents. Given the universality of the telephone and increasing police reliance on patrol cars, most of these requests to police agencies are

made by telephone rather than directly to an officer working 'on the street'. While estimates would vary across communities, it is generally agreed that responding to calls for service constitutes the bulk of the police workload in all agencies.

2 *Scheduled requests* for general patterns of service in response to vested interests and/or chronic situations. These tend to be made directly to city or agency representatives by groups or individuals and are seldom made by calling a police operator.

3 *Organisationally produced demand.* Independent of specific calls for service, the police may initiate investigative action, surveillance, arrests, raids or other strategic actions in response to some perceived problem (Goldstein, 1979). In so doing, the police may be responding to their *own* perceptions of problems in the community (e.g., a rapid rise in rapes, purse snatchings or drug use). Such problems may not have been articulated by citizens.

Typically, the nature of the demands, which we refer to as the 'service demand structure', has been explained in terms of the demographic characteristics of the community in question. Our argument is not with the use of demographic variables as indicators of the service demand structure. In fact, we believe that used properly, they can serve as one important type of predictor of the needs for police service. Our concern is that the most commonly used demographic variables limit our understanding of the demand structure, and its impact on service delivery and outcomes such as cost and effectiveness.

For example, we logically assume that the cost of police service reflects, in part, a response to the policing needs of the jurisdiction. There is evidence that population size is positively associated with the cost of police service. And yet, what is it about the size of a population that generates 'demands' for police service? We cannot answer that question with high correlations between 'population size' and numbers of police or levels of expenditures. We cannot learn from these correlations the various types of policing needs that are generated by differing population characteristics. In fact, a static measure like 'city size' may mask several population characteristics which might affect directly the types of services needed by the city. Such 'masked' variables could include: rate of population growth or decline, age distribution, racial/ethnic mix (or the change in same), economic and employment patterns, population dispersion or density, etc.

As one example, we can consider 'percentage elderly', a demographic factor found to relate positively to *per capita* police expenditures and manpower. One reason for such a correlation may be found in recent research on the correlates of crime incident reporting (cf.

Hindelang, 1976; Skogan, 1974). Elderly citizens are more likely than younger citizens to notify the police about a criminal incident. In addition to crime related services, it seems likely that elderly residents are more likely to generate medical emergency services calls, whether these calls are related to deaths, injuries or acute conditions such as heart attacks. A large elderly population is likely to lead to a higher than average investment in funeral escort services. By contrast, a relatively young population would generate attendant problems.

The point is that a finer specification of the population permits us to link particular types and levels of service to community characteristics in ways that more globally defined predictors do not.

The same argument can be made for indicators of jurisdiction land use. A correlation between the business/residential land use ratio and the police service levels or costs tell us nothing as to which kinds of businesses generate which types of service demands. Presumably a shopping centre and an industrial park may present different demands. Similarly, after-hours entertainment districts or recreational sites may generate other kinds of demands. Certainly, the size and nature of the private security industry in the community would affect the type and number of demands transmitted to the public police agency. So, too, would the type and extent of functional overlapping of public police agencies within an area.

Similarly, land use patterns tell us nothing about the types of needs associated with differing residential patterns. Apartment block areas may present a different demand structure than do 'bedsit' type areas. Similarly, both the 'length of residency' and 'age/quality of housing' patterns for an area may generate varying service demands and 'felt needs'.

The common land use measures do not allow us to identify, for example, the types of service required for abandoned warehouses, parks, beaches, hospitals, highways, tourist attractions, etc.

The same can be said of indicators of relationships between the jurisdiction and surrounding areas. For example, we do not know what services are required by small surrounding communities which may not provide their own specialised police services. We do not know what types of services are required by suburban residents using the city for work and recreation. Conversely, the concentration of work places, entertainment and recreational centres in contiguous jurisdictions may establish traffic flow patterns as well as opportunities for crime so as to influence allocation of police and the nature of services provided by the central community.

Using the more refined measures of community and population characteristics, we could address such questions as: what changes in amount of police time or type of police services are administered to residential areas that increase in non-white population; what service allocation changes result from jurisdictions or areas within jurisdictions becoming more or less densely populated or repopulated by more or less dependent citizens, or repopulated by age groups whose rate of criminal activity is higher? How does service demand and allocation relate to land use? In effect, to understand and predict police service as it relates to changing community and population conditions, we need to identify empirically the 'service demand structure' of police jurisdictions. The only way to do this is through research which allows calls for service to be tied directly to the characteristics of the callers and service recipients and to the physical characteristics of the location of the incident. This type of data will avoid the ecological fallacies that can result from predicting the service demand from community-wide demographic data and will allow accurate prediction of the changing content of the police role. This, in turn, will provide for rational police planning of selection, training, strategies and budgets.

Role enactment

Knowing only the *content* of the role (the jobs police are expected to do), tells us nothing about the way in which the job is performed. Research on police roles indicates that while role content has been described, almost no work has been done to assess the quality of role enactment. This is understandable in terms of the very complex and demanding measurement and value issues that must be resolved in order to evaluate performance. Nevertheless, we will argue that this is currently one of the most critical items on the research agenda. It is only the measurement of the quality of performance or service delivery which will produce an understanding of why desired organisational outcomes are or are not achieved.

By this we do not suggest that quality performance will always result in desired outcomes. Given the conflicting role expectations and the complex field in which police operate, it will often be the case that someone's desired outcome will not be achieved. But, while quality performance should be oriented to obtaining goals, a good performance is its own outcome. The civil, humane and responsible handling of people is an end in itself, even when it leads to nothing else.

What do we mean by the quality of performance? Two levels will be described: individual and organisational.

The inability to measure quality police performance at an individual

48

level is perhaps one of the most serious and perplexing problems facing police researchers and practitioners. After two generations of research on police roles, task analyses, studies on productivity, we still cannot specify what police do in handling specific situations or measure the effect of what they do. Consequently, we have no empirical basis for evaluating what they do or for saying what they should do.

Ironically, the specification of 'good' performance received early emphasis in police research during the late 1960s. Mort Bard's work on managing domestic disputes (Bard, 1974; Bard, et al., 1970), was original and creative. Although attempts to institutionalise programmes of managing domestic disputes through conflict resolution techniques have encountered many difficulties, that is no reason to downplay its importance conceptually and empirically. Bard documented police officer response, identified patterns of responses which, for a variety of reasons, were judged to be preferable, then trained officers in those responses and finally measured the effect. While we might quibble with Bard's evaluation of the effectiveness of conflict resolution techniques, the process he used to understand what was being done and to develop alternate modes of treatment was important and appropriate for studying the impact of service delivery (whether policing, casework, counselling, psychotherapy, whatever). But it ended there. This promising beginning should have been the first step in the careful delineation of police responses to particular clusters of incidents (handling drunks, mentally ill, victims, etc.), identification of preferable responses and, finally, measurement of the impact of those responses.

We are not sure why this work was never built upon. The Police Foundation tried to use it to measure officer performance in the evaluation of the Dallas Human Resource Development Program (Kelling and Wycoff, 1978), but the problems that developed in the programme forced us to settle for use of many of the surrogate and commonly used standard measure of individual officer performance (administrative record information). (Unfortunately, it seems that measurement of performance has tended to be tied to evaluating programmes. We argue that programme evaluation will continue to be made much more difficult until we deal with these significant measurement issues independent of programme evaluations.) Also, flashier research like the Kansas City Preventive Patrol Experiment (Kelling, et al., 1974), the response time studies (Bieck, 1977 a, b, c; Pate, et al., 1976), and the Rand study (Greenwood and Petersilia, 1975), of investigative effectiveness, came along to dominate the attention of both practitioners and researchers, leading to professional debate and consumption of resources. But probably the more important cause is the fact that research into actual performance measures involves an extremely tedious measurement problem, which in its early stages does not lend itself to relatively inexpensive solutions. The costs of such research are very high. If we are going to do the job properly, the issue of the outcome of performance is an independent problem which will have to be worked on simultaneously and, for a complete understanding of the problem, ultimately linked with measures of performance.

Performance itself apart from outcomes must be the primary object of interest. Initially, the focus will have to be on identifying the range of behaviours officers use in dealing with incident types, making judgements about what behaviours officers use in dealing with incident types, making judgements about what behaviours they ought to use by dealing with value considerations, thinking creatively and borrowing from other service delivery approaches, training officers to use specified behaviours, and finally, on the organisational 'fixing' of those behaviours in field settings. (Organisationally 'fixed' behaviour is that which is well integrated into personal and agency norms, is supervised and rewarded.) Only then can the relationship between those behaviours and outcomes be examined experimentally. Previous evaluation research has often attempted to evaluate newly prescribed performances before they were organisationally fixed. At the present time, researchers and evaluators have had so much experience with programmes not 'taking hold' or lasting beyond the beginning phase that the belief that professional behaviour can be experimented with in settings that offer no reward for that kind of 'deviant' performance and in settings which in fact will probably punish creativity ought by now to be fairly well eradicated.

A second reason why this work has not been done is that it is easy for researchers and funding agencies to assume that such measures have been developed previously. The phrase 'performance evaluation' has been in use several years now. So much money had been spent on task analyses, role analyses, productivity studies, etc., that we may take for granted that this work has produced measures of quality performance. It is easy to overlook the fact that this work has focused on the content and consequence of roles while ignoring role process and performance. We remain uninformed about police behaviour.

The consequences of this failure to develop measures and our self-deception about our failures have been enormous. The result is an impasse in critical areas of police research. Examples of this impasse are to be found in the area of the selection of police officers, the impact of education on the delivery of police service, the measurement of organisational effectiveness and the development of cost benefit analysis. We will briefly discuss each of these.

1 *The selection of police officers.* In the United States, civil rights legislation and litigation have led to numerous efforts to develop officer selection standards and procedures (Rosenfeld and Thornton, 1976; Furcon and Fromel, 1973). The final step in all such efforts involves the validation of the standards/procedures against some performance criteria. Unlike industrial applications, the performance criteria for such efforts are created concurrently with the development of the selection instruments. The criteria generally involve judgements made by raters (usually supervisors) who have little opportunity actually to observe officers as they conduct their jobs and who do not share common definitions of what good police service involves. Hence, such validation efforts generally leave the reader with a hollow 'is that all there is?' feeling. We endorse Campbell's (1976) position in his recent review of the performance criterion literature. He suggests, for example, that if dealing with domestic disputes is an important aspect of police work 'then a scale should be constructed that will permit that part of a policeman's performance to be rated; and the different levels of performance from very good to very poor should be defined as clearly and meaningfully as possible'.

2 *The impact of education on the delivery of police services.* One of the major reform efforts in policing during the 1960s and 1970s in the US involved recruiting better educated police officers. It was believed that college educated officers would be more qualified than less educated counterparts to handle the complex job of the police officer. A number of efforts to assess the veracity of this assumption have used officer attitudes as indicators of the quality of police service delivery (Miller and Fry, 1976; Regoli, 1976; Smith and Ostrom, 1973; Wycoff and Susmilch, 1978). Other efforts have utilised organisationally recorded indicators of performance, such as commendations, complaints, sick days and supervisor ratings as indicators of officer performance (Cohen and Chaiken, 1973; Gascio, 1977; Weirman, 1978).

In reviewing this literature on the impact of college education on policing, Wycoff and Susmilch (1978) conclude that such measures tell us little about the actual outcome of concern (i.e., the quality of service) and recommend that additional resources not be invested in trying to verify the importance of education until measures of the quality of police service are developed.

3 *Measures of organisational effectiveness.* We have discussed elsewhere the problems associated with using response time and passings (the number of times a patrol car passes a given point) as measures of organisational effectiveness (Kelling, 1978). Both of

these are process variables which assume a direct link between them and actual output (response time leads to more apprehensions, increased citizen satisfaction, etc., and number of passings deters crime, etc.). While such assumed linkages may be logical, they clearly have not been established empirically. In fact, the linkage between response time and its assumed outputs has been fairly well undermined (this will be discussed in more detail later).

Besides response time, two other indicators of outcomes have been commonly used to evaluate police agencies. These are citizen satisfaction and reported crime. Both indicators present serious measurement and interpretation problems and we would like to discuss them in some detail.

(a)   *Citizen satisfaction.* Citizen's attitudes have been extensively used as measures of organisation effectiveness (Ostrom, 1976; Ostrom, et al., 1976). Generally, questions are designed to assess citizen satisfaction with services, citizen estimates of response time and citizen fear of crime. These are then utilised as measures of quality. While the quality of policing may have an impact on such variables, we believe that it is conceptually and methodologically incorrect to equate such variables with the quality of service. It would seem unreasonable to expect citizens to judge officers' performance when, generally, they are not even aware of police practices. A substantial proportion of citizens have few or no recent contacts with police. Further, a sample of households is a very restricted one which cannot represent the attitudes of non-residents using area streets, merchants and small business people who have a tremendous investment in communities, unemployed street people, and staff members and consumers of schools, recreational units and community organisations. The responses of all these groups are as important as, and perhaps even more relevant than, the responses of a random selection of households. Additionally, the Kansas City study suggested that citizens surveyed on a random household basis cannot even distinguish changes in the quantity of police services, let alone their quality. Additionally, it is conceivable that citizens may be 'satisfied' when local police illegally harass unwanted visitors in business or residential areas, or they may be 'satisfied' when local police differentially enforce traffic laws for residents and non-residents. Citizens may be 'dissatisfied' with police because the police may have legitimately exercised authority against them (delivered a summons, issued a citation, requested that a noisy party be quieted). In each of these examples, the quality of police service is inversely related to citizen satisfaction and the meaning of citizen attitudes becomes very difficult to interpret for policing purposes.

(b)   *Reported crime.* Reported crime has been a popular indicator of crime levels and measure of organisational effectiveness. (For a more extensive discussion of this issue, see Bottomley and Coleman's chapter in this volume). An overriding problem with this measure is the question of which behaviours are defined as criminal and when. An action may occur which is in fact criminal but which is not defined as such. An attack, or a threat of one, by a friend or relative may simply be thought of as a disagreement whereas, under strict interpretation of the law, it could be defined as a criminal offence. Forgery, shoplifting and various forms of 'white-collar crime' may occur without the victim ever being aware of it.

Even if an action is defined as criminal, information about it must be provided to the police before that action can be officially recorded. Except in the very few cases in which crimes are disco-vered by the police themselves (an estimated 1.6 per cent of personal robberies and 0.4 per cent of household burglaries, for example, are discovered by police (Skogan, 1976), crimes come to the attention of the police by citizen reporting. The result is that it is difficult to determine the extent to which the amount of reported crime represents the amount of actual crime.

Crimes may go unreported because victims may feel that nothing can be done about the incident; be embarrassed by the incident; want private revenge; fear their assailant; be afraid of the police; find reporting inconvenient; etc.

Even if a crime is reported, there are many circumstances in which the victim may distort the incident for his or her own interest. A victim may exaggerate the value of stolen property; fabricate the loss of property; neglect to mention ways in which his/her actions constituted negligence or even liability in the inci-dent; may alter the description of the incident in order to avoid personal embarrassment; etc.

Once a report, however accurate, of a victimisation has been given to the police, it is not automatically entered into the offi-cial crime statistics. In fact, two recent research studies indicate that the police are as likely to record reported crime as citizens are to report actual crime, (Skogan, 1976).

There are many reasons why the police may fail to record a reported crime. An officer may decide that the victim's claim is false; decide that the citizen's complaint is perfectly legitimate but does not involve the breaking of the law; conclude that the reported incident, although apparently involving a crime, is one for which only minimal or no evidence exists; etc. Many incidents are resolved at the scene by the police officer. In such cases, pro-secution would be pointless and, therefore, recording may seem unnecessary. Assaults between family members and neighbours or disputes between landlords and tenants are frequently 'handled by the officer' (the official disposition in many cities) in this way.

An officer may face certain organisational pressures which affect whether it seems desirable to file an official crime report.

Such power to manipulate recorded crime may be used by police to address specific organisational demands and problems faced by an officer. For example, an officer may not record a crime in which a prominent civic leader is alleged to be the perpetrator. Charges made against police officers as suspects may not be readily recorded. Allegations of criminality which, if they were prosecuted, would reveal undercover police operations will often go unrecorded. The same may also be true of crimes which would reveal non-police informants.

The reporting and recording rates, of course, are not independent but work in a multiplicative fashion. If one accepts the conclusions of the speculative analysis of National Crime Survey data in the United States, approximately 40 per cent of crimes are reported and about 50 per cent of these are recorded (Skogan, 1976). Multiplying these two rates, only 20 per cent of crimes which actually occur fully appear in official statistics. If one accepts the more rigorously derived estimates of Sparks, et al., both the reporting and the recording rates are about 30 per cent (Skogan, 1976, p. 155). Multiplying these, one finds that only 9 per cent of crimes are recorded.

4 *Cost benefit analyses.* The issue of cost benefit analyses will be discussed quite briefly. We now believe that we are at the point where we can begin to identify the costs of police services within reasonable ranges. Even calculating cost is problematic, however. It is practically impossible in the US to get accurate city budget figures (one gets at least three or four 'accurate' budget figures both for city income and expenditures; the number of city employees changes depending on what document is looked at; etc.). The result is that calculated costs can vary extremely widely depending on what figures are used. Yet if one is careful to identify data sources and how the calculations are biased (taking upper or lower levels of reported data), presenting the trade-offs between strategy options can be powerful and persuasive. As difficult as it is to calculate costs associated with units of service, it is self-deceptive to believe that we can go from calculations of cost to cost benefit analysis. Not having firm measures of quality limits us to costing out units of service. We simply do not have units of benefit (product) against which we can allocate costs.

We are struggling with this issue now in a study of foot patrol. One of the primary arguments against foot patrol in the US is its high costs. We suspect that, at best, we will be able to indicate the costs of various service units when delivered by foot or automobile. Our attempts to cost out benefits will be frustrated by the lack of indicators of the quality of service delivery.

In addition to the four research impasses which have just been discussed, the lack of measures of performance quality leaves police administrators unable to develop rational schemes to evaluate officers, creates difficulty for developing training relevant to incidents, and makes it difficult to guide officers to behaviour which is organisationally desirable. Agencies are unable to specify what officers do in incidents rather than what they should not do.

In sum, surrogate measures have been developed to measure the quality of organisational or individual performance. These surrogate measures may or may not reflect actual performance. If we are properly to evaluate police services and adjust police responses to changing circumstances, either measures must be developed which actually measure the extent and quality of the police services provided, or research must be conducted to validate the surrogate measures now used.

Role capacity

Role capacity refers to the organisational and individual resources that can be used to create a role enactment in response to a demand We shall argue that the existence of any given capacity does not lead automatically to a given performance or to a desired organisa-outcome.

For police, the capacity to perform consists of organisational structures, strategies, technology, policies, personnel, supervision, reward structures, legal constraints and others. For purpose of illustration, our discussion will focus on technology and strategies.

Technology

The development of technology has had great impact on how police services are delivered in the United States. Technology provided call boxes and handcuffs, and later the patrol car, one-way radios, burglar alarms, helicopters, computer-aided dispatch, and finally the automatic vehicle locator system. Each new advance in technology has been heralded by enthusiastic belief that it would revolutionise the effectiveness of the police in apprehending criminals.

The advent of the use of police radios and automobiles was generally hailed as a dramatic development in law enforcement technology, which would give police the extra 'edge' on criminals.

The one-way radio, and later the two and three-way radios were to translate the manoeuverability of motorised patrol into a 'striking power', rendering call boxes obsolete. Two-way radios coupled with burglar alarms would allow for rapid response to commercial burglaries and robberies resulting in increased on-scene apprehensions.

A more contemporary example of the belief in the efficacy of computer-based police technology is found in Doering, (1975):

> Within three minutes, the nearest patrol unit sights the suspect's car and a short time later the first suspect is apprehended. A second patrol unit converging on the area picks up the second suspect. Both have some of the reported loot and as they are brought to headquarters it appears that the case is well on the way to being solved thanks to the quick response time, the computer's memory and a well-executed tactical plan.

After a discussion of command and control operations, the author concludes:

> In summary the design and technological know-how exists to upgrade the Command/Control capability of any police department to the degree of sophistication required to effectively meet the tactical requirements. It needs only to be accepted and practiced.

However, in spite of this pervasive belief in the efficacy of technologically-based police strategies, recent empirical evidence has failed to support the high expectations of its proponents. Preventive patrol has been unable to demonstrate conclusive results (Kelling et al., 1974). Rapid response to calls for service seems to have little effect, (Bieck, 1977a, b, c; Pate, et al., 1976). Aside from the questionable value of short response time, automatic vehicle locator systems do not as yet reduce it (Larson, et al., 1978).

Moreover, in spite of computerisation, there is no notably greater accuracy of reported crime figures than there was 20 to 30 years ago. Even the administrative use of the computer to store and retrieve departmental data seems not to have been too successful. Recently, a series of murders terrorised citizens of New York City for a long period of time. Later, when the murderer was apprehended, a detective indicated he could have made an identification more quickly if the information had *not* been stored in the computer, (*New York Post*, 1972). The attitude of many in policing seems to be that the adoption of technological advancements has been ineffective and expensive, but at least harmless. The various commission reports which assume technology's ultimate usefulness also assume its proper and skilful use and even this has yet to be systematically demonstrated.

However, it is by no means universally accepted that the adoption of technological devices is as neutral as its advocates assume. Some argue that the use of automobiles, first without radios, and then automobiles with one and two-way radios, then heated and air-conditioned cars, then cars with computer terminals, has substantially changed how the police relate to citizens, to each other and to the police organisation itself. The argument goes on, that as technology intruded, the police developed into an emergency response system, not only responding to citizens' calls for service, but also to alarm systems.

The problem with the use of technology and our research into it is that we have not conceived of technology in terms of the entire demand structure for police services. As presently used, technology—the capacity to do—encourages organisational drift to handling those police functions for which technology, at least theoretically, is helpful. (Put another way, it is the law of the instrument: 'Give a small boy a hammer, and it should come as no surprise that for those problems he encounters he will use as a solution those means most available to him—pounding'.) The result may be that some portion of the demand structure goes unanswered. Thus, the clamour for foot patrol in more and more US cities can be seen as a demand for services which directly conflicts with rapid response to all calls, this latter which we conceive to be an organisationally induced demand—rapid response to all calls for service.

Police strategies

A parallel situation is to be found in the research into police strategies. During their 150 years of formal existence, police departments have devised various patrol strategies of achieving their goals. Despite nuances and complexities, these strategies of preventive patrol can be summarised as follows:

1 *Undirected patrol:* also called random, routine or traditional, this strategy consists of patrol cars driving about in an unsystematic fashion, supposedly with the result that criminals are deterred from committing crimes and law-abiding citizens are reassured by the visible omnipresence of law enforcement officers.

2 *Directed patrol:* sometimes called aggressive patrol (Wilson and Boland, 1978), crime-attack patrol (Wilson, 1968), specialised patrol (Webb, 1977a, b), high-impact anti-crime programmes (Chelimsky, 1976a, b; Dahmann, 1974), or by any of several other names, this approach involves the assignment of officers to specific locations for the explicit purpose of preventing specific crimes. This might involve the assumption of disguises, the driving

of unmarked patrol vehicles, the creation of a highly visible patrol presence, carrying out stakeouts in crime-ridden places, making frequent stops and investigations of pedestrians and drivers or any of several other approaches designed to affect specific crime patterns.

3 *Community-oriented patrol:* whether called 'community service policing' (Wilson, 1968) 'team policing' (Gay and Woodward, 1977; Gay, et al., 1977a; Schwartz and Clarren, 1977; Schwartz and Clarren, 1978; Sherman, et al., 1973), 'beat commander project' (Bloch and Specht, 1973), the 'basic car plan' (Sherman, et al., 1973; Gay, 1977a), the 'neighbourhood police team' (Sherman, et al., 1973; Cho, 1974), or 'community-based policing' (Gay, et al., 1977a, Wasson, 1975; Germann, 1969), this approach involves a general identification of the police with a specific area, its people and their concerns and interests, and a decentralisation of decision-making.

4 *Arrest-oriented patrol:* whatever the label, this approach focuses on the apprehension of suspects as a way of preventing crime. Rather than simply deterring, or perhaps displacing crime, the goal is to remove potential criminals from the scene, thereby making it impossible for them to commit crimes.

Briefly we will review the research in each of these areas.

Undirected patrol. The Kansas City Preventive Patrol Experiment suggested that reducing or increasing the level of preventive patrol (driving, more or less randomly, in an area in order to maintain police visibility and therefore deter crime and reduce citizen fear) had no noticeable effect. Zimring, (1978), taking the critiques of the study into account, concludes that at least this conservative inference is justified: 'increasing preventive patrol by a factor of two or more for 12 months in car-patrolled areas similar to those studied probably does not reduce the incidence of crime to a great extent'. A study by Schnelle, et al., (1977), tends to support this conclusion. Other studies, often cited in discussions of the effect of patrol on crime actually concern intense, specialised or directed strategies rather than the nondirected patrol tested in Kansas City.

Directed patrol. Although several departments have implemented various types of specialised patrol programmes (Boydstun, 1975; Pate, et al., 1976; Schack, 1977; Ward, et al., 1975; Webb, et al., 1977a), recent summary analysis by Webb, et al., (1977a). concludes: '... there have been too few evaluations of specialised patrols and those which have been done are often of a quality unacceptable to the research community'.

Community-oriented patrol. Up to 60 departments have instituted some variant of this strategy, basically involving decentralisation of decision making, maximum interaction and identification with citizens in a certain area, sometimes incorporating aspects of the directed patrol approach or the arrest-oriented strategy. Although several studies and reviews (Bloch and Specht, 1973; Boydstun and Sherry, 1975; Gay, et al., 1977a, b; Gourley, 1954; Marx and Archer, 1972; Myren, 1972; Schwartz and Clarren, 1977; Schwartz and Clarren, 1978; Sherman, et al., 1973; Washnis, 1976; Waskow, 1967), have been conducted, Gay, et al., (1977), conclude that: 'Evaluation studies of team policing have been few in number and varying in quality'. No convincing evaluation, therefore, of community-oriented patrol can be said to exist.

Arrest-oriented patrol. Although several studies (Avio and Clark, 1976; 1978; Bailey, unpublished; Black, 1970; Block, 1972; Chapman, et al., 1975; Chapman, 1976; Cho, 1974; Cramer, 1978; Furlong and Mehay, 1978; Greenberg, et al., 1978; Greenwood and Wadycki, 1973; Jones, 1973; Krajick, 1978; Levine, 1975; McPheters and Stronge, 1974; Mehay, 1974; Mehay and Furlong, 1978; Morris and Tweeten, 1971; Municipal Performance Report, 1973, O'Connor and Gilman, 1978; Phillips, et al., 1976; Pogue, 1975; Reppetto, 1975; Swimmer, F., 1974; Swimmer, G., 1974; Thaler, 1977, Votey and Phillips, 1975; Wellford, 1975; Wilson and Boland, 1978; Zimring, 1978) have conducted cross sectional analyses of the deterrent effect of police arrest behaviour, no well evaluated studies of the effectiveness of this strategy exist. Much research has been conducted recently, however, that indicates that most crimes are solved, if at all, through the use of information provided to the responding officer, (Chaiken, 1975; Greenwood, et al., 1977). Such programmes as Cleveland Heights Patrol Emphasis Program (Gay, 1977b), Wilmington's Split Force Experiment (Tien, et al., 1978), the Syracuse Crime Control Teams (Elliott, 1978), and Rochester's Co-ordinated Team Policing (Bloch and Bell, 1976; Bloch and Ulberg, 1972; Bloch and Ulberg, 1975), have shown that patrol officers can successfully conduct investigations. The possibilities, then, of arrest-oriented patrol have begun to be explored; an evaluation of its effects is not yet available.

Apart from studies into these strategies, other discrete police practices have been studied. Police departments in Kansas City, Cleveland Heights, Wilmington and elsewhere have found that, by implementing the suggestions made by Gay, et al., 1977a, and Chaiken, 1975a, and others, officers could be allocated proportionately, over time and space, and thereby produce a more efficient patrol operation.

Various departments, including St Louis, Kansas City, New Haven and others, have found that there are alternative ways to handle calls rather than routinely dispatching a patrol car. More recent research, not yet released, indicates that citizens are willing to accept such alternatives. Further support for adopting such alternative approaches is supported by the work of Pate, et al. (1976), Bieck (1977a, b, c), with the Kansas City Police Department and the Wilmington study, (Tien, et al., 1978), which conclude that citizens are willing to accept longer response times if they are given realistic expectations. The Kansas City study (Bertram and Vargo, 1976; Bieck, 1977a, b, c), furthermore, finds that citizens often wait so long before reporting a crime that a hurried police response is fruitless.

Once a call is responded to, other research (Bloch and Bell, 1976; Bloch and Ulberg, 1972; Bloch and Ulberg, 1975; Bloch and Weidman, 1975; Eck, 1978; Greenberg, 1976; Heller and McEwen, 1973), indicates a department can make considerable strides toward reducing its investigatory workload. This work indicates that by using such criteria as seriousness and 'solvability factors', the number of cases that receive prolonged attention can be greatly limited.

A study in San Diego (Boydstun, 1977), compared the relative effectiveness of one/two officer vehicles and found that one-officer cars are more cost effective than, and at least as safe as, two-officer cars. This finding has been further supported by the Split-Force Experiment in Wilmington.

Notice the thrust of all these studies. They focus on where police officers are, how fast they get there, how many of them there are, and how they are organised. For all practical purposes, none deal with what police officers do in handling incidents and what effect their actions have. It is almost as if policing were an automated vending machine of services, with officer performance discounted as a 'human factor', a mere electrical noise in an otherwise perfect system.

Looking back on our own work, the Kansas City experiment was an important and interesting study. And while it did measure the impact of patrol on what police said it would affect, primarily crime, it did not deal with other critical areas of demand for police services or quality of police performance. In that respect, it was fairly uni-dimensional. Even if preventive patrol had proved effective, the study would not have addressed the issue of whether preventive patrol should continue. If preventive patrol had had a significant effect on crime, it might have been at the cost of ignoring important demands for service and reducing the quality of some of the services that were delivered. Future research should focus on the relationship of police strategy (the capacity to do) with what the demand structure is and

and with quality police performance (what police do). To do anything less is to reduce greatly the significance of what we can learn.

Role outcomes

Outcome refers to the impact an officer has when handling an incident or the effect the organisation has on a defined problem. It becomes immediately clear from the earlier discussion that outcome (individual and agency effectiveness) is linked to demand, quality performance and the capacity to perform. Effectiveness in dealing with any situation or problem must be defined by reconciling what are often conflicting demands, the restraints of legality and civility implicit in quality performance and the restraints imposed by the capacity to perform. Analyses of effectiveness which do not take these factors into account do not allow the organisation or individuals to modify their performance to become more effective. For example, the capacity to perform (i.e., technology) always has to be filtered through, and use of it adjusted to, quality performance. The fact that an organisation develops a capacity to do a particular thing which might lead to significant crime reduction does not guarantee that the organisation will be able to achieve that outcome. Conflicting demands and the restraints of quality performance may so mute the impact of the technological capacity that it ultimately has no effect. The consequence of finding no effect might lead one to conclude that that particular capacity cannot lead to the desired outcome. In fact, this might not be the case at all. The capacity might lead to the desired outcome once it was manifest in improved quality of performance. Implementation failure might have prevented the capacity from being translated into better performance and hence into improved outcomes. The researcher who failed to measure the quality of performance would not have known this and would have erroneously concluded that the capacity was in and of itself incapable of resulting in the desired outcome. The real problem missed by the researcher might be with the process of translation rather than inherent in the capacity.

Conclusion

We would argue that most of the research conducted on police in the United States has focused on the *capacity* to perform and on *outcomes*. The issues of what the police ought to do (the content) and how they ought to do it (the performance) and of how these interact with the capacity to perform, remain for the most part un-examined. At best we have static and insufficient understanding of demand and highly suspect surrogate indicators of quality performance. Yet to look at any one of these research issues separately is to provide only one segment of the information about policing which is needed to develop rational policies. To know the nature and origin of the service demand, for example, is still to know nothing about the way in which the requested services are actually delivered. If the desire is to upgrade police service delivery, it is essential to know the relationship between selection and training criteria and role *performance.* Obviously, this requires measures of the quality of service delivery. To date, efforts to validate police selection and training standards have been based primarily on studies of role *content.* Unfortunately, knowledge of the nature of the job does not inform us automatically about what is required to perform the job well. Nor does an understanding of the way in which a job presently is performed tell us automatically how that job should be performed. Role studies and task analyses are not prescriptive. Certainly, the first step is a job analysis which helps us understand the nature of the demand, but it is only the first step. The second, and equally essential, is to define and develop measurement of quality performance as it relates to that demand.

The point is that the interaction between demand, quality, capacity and outcome is so complex and intricate that we cannot understand one without the others. If we are to know why we have a particular outcome, or lack of it, it must come out of an understanding of these interactions. Each separate body of information is critical but each, standing alone, provides insufficient information for the organisation that wishes to evaluate and modify itself. Only with attention to the total, integrated research agenda can we hope through research to provide the information necessary for the rational development of policy in policing.

References

Avio, K. L., and Clark, C. S., (1976), *Property Crime in Canada: An Econometric Study,* University of Toronto Press, Toronto.

Avio, K. L., and Clark, C. S., (1978), 'The supply of property offences in Ontario: evidence on the deterrent effect of punishment', *Canadian Journal of Economics,* 11, pp. 1—19.

Bailey, W. C., (unpublished) 'Certainty of arrest and crime rates for major felonies', Cleveland State University (mimeo).

Bard, M., (1974) Implications of collaboration between law enforcement and the social sciences', *FBI Law Enforcement Bulletin,* July.

Bard, M., Zacker, and Rutter, (1970), *Training Police as Specialists in Family Crisis Intervention,* Report to the National Institute of Law Enforcement and Criminal Justice, US Government Printing Office, Washington, DC.

Bercal, T. E., (1970), 'Calls for police assistance', *American Behavioral Scientist,* 13, pp. 681–92.

Bertram, D. K., and Vargo, A., (1976), 'Response time analysis study: preliminary findings on robbery in Kansas City', *Police Chief,* 43, pp. 74–7.

Bieck, W., (1977a), *Response Time Analysis: Executive Summary,* Kansas City, Missouri Police Department, Kansas City, Mo.

Bieck, W., (1977b), *Response Time Analysis, vol. I, Methodology,* Law Enforcement Assistance Administration, Washington, DC.

Bieck, W., (1977c), *Response Time Analysis, vol. II, Analysis,* Law Enforcement Assistance Administration, Washington, DC.

Black, D. J., (1970), 'Production of crime rates', *American Sociological Review,* 35, pp. 733–48.

Bloch, M. K., (1972), 'An Economic Analysis of Theft with Special Emphasis on Household Decisions Under Uncertainty', dissertation, Stanford University.

Bloch, P. B., and Bell, J., (1976), *Managing Investigations: The Rochester System,* Police Foundation, Washington, DC.

Bloch, P. B., and Specht, D., (1973), *Neighborhood Team Policing,* US Government Printing Office, Washington, DC.

Bloch, P. B., and Ulberg, C., (1972), 'The beat commander concept', *The Police Chief,* September.

Bloch, P., and Ulberg, C., (1975), *Auditing Clearance Rates,* Police Foundation, Washington, DC.

Bloch, P., and Weidman, D., (1975), *Managing Criminal Investigations,* The Urban Institute, Washington, DC.

Boydstun, J. E., (1975), *San Diego Field Interrogation. Final Report,* Police Foundation, Washington, DC.

Boydstun, J. E., (1977), *Patrol Staffing in San Diego: One or Two-Officer Units,* Police Foundation, Washington, DC.

Boydstun, J. E., and Sherry, M. E., (1975), *San Diego Community Profile. Final Report,* Police Foundation, Washington, DC.

California Commission on Peace Officer Standards and Training, (1978), *Entry-Level Law Enforcement Officer Job Analysis.*

Campbell, J. P., (1976), 'The Assessment and Prediction of Police Performance', University of Minnesota (mimeo).

Chaiken, J. M., (1975a), *Patrol Allocation Methodology for Police Departments,* Rand Institute, Santa Monica, Calif.

Chaiken, J. M., (1975b), *The Criminal Investigation Process, vol. II,*

Survey of Municipal and County Police Departments, (R-1777-DOJ), Rand Institute, Santa Monica, Calif. (Revised version in Greenwood, P., Chaiken, J., and Petersilia, J., (1977), *The Criminal Investigation Process,* D. C. Heath, Lexington, Mass.)

Chapman, J., Hirsch, W., and Sonenblum, S., (1975), 'Crime prevention, the police production function and budgeting', *Public Finance,* 30, pp. 17—215.

Chapman, J., (1976), 'An economic model of crime and police: some empirical results', *Journal of Research in Crime and Delinquency,* 13, pp. 48-63.

Chelimsky, E., (1976a), *High Impact Anti-Crime Program, vol. I, National Level Evaluation,* Law Enforcement Assistance Administration, Washington, DC.

Chelimsky, E., (1976b), *High Impact Anti-Crime Program, vol. II, National Level Evaluation: Final Report,* Law Enforcement Assistance Administration, Washington, DC.

Cho, Y., (1974), *Public Policy and Urban Crime,* Ballinger Publishing Co., Cambridge, Mass.

Cohen, B., and Chaiken, J. M., (1973), *Police Background Characteristics and Performance,* Lexington Books, Lexington, Mass.

Cramer, J. A., (1978), *Preventing Crime,* Sage Publications, Beverly Hills, Calif.

Cumming, E., Cumming, L., and Edell, L., (1965), 'Policeman as philosopher, guide and friend', *Social Problems,* 12, pp. 276—86.

Dahmann, J. S., (1974), *High Impact Anti-Crime Program: A Review of Six Research Studies on the Relationship Between Police Patrol Activity and Crime,* The Mitre Corporation, Washington, DC.

Doering, R. D., (1975), 'Engineering perspective on police department command and control operations', in Bopp, W. J., (ed.), *Police Administration: Selected Readings,* Holbrook Press, Boston, Mass.

Eck, J. E., (1978), *Burglary Investigation Decision Model Replication: A Multi-Site Evaluation,* Presented to LEAA National Workshop on Criminal Justice Evaluation, November.

Elliott, J. F., (1978), 'Crime control teams: an alternative to the conventional operational procedure of investigating crimes', *Journal of Criminal Justice,* 6, pp. 11—23.

Furcon, J., and Fromel, E. C., (1973), *Relation of Selected Psychological Tests to Measure Police Job Performance in Illinois,* Illinois Department of Personnel.

Furlong, W. J., and Mehay, S. L., (1978), *The Deterrent Effect of Urban Police Services: Empirical Results for Canada,* Meeting of Southern Economic Association, Washington, DC, November.

Gascio, W. F., (1977), 'Formal education and police officer performance', *Journal of Police Science and Administration,* 5, pp. 89—96.

Gay, W. G., (1977a), *Improving Patrol Productivity, vol. I, Routine Patrol,* Law Enforcement Assistance Administration, Washington, DC.

Gay, W. G., (1977b), *Patrol Emphasis Evaluation. Cleveland Heights, Ohio,* University City Science Centre, Philadelphia, Penn.

Gay, W. G., Day, H. T., and Woodward, J. P., (1977a), *Neighborhood Team Policing,* Law Enforcement Assistance Administration, Washington, DC.

Gay, W. G., Day, H. T., and Woodward, J. P., (1977b), *Issues in Team Policing: A Review of the Literature,* Law Enforcement Assistance Administration, Washington, DC.

Germann, A. C.,(1969), 'Community policing: an assessment', *Journal of Criminal Law, Criminology and Police Science,* 60, pp. 89—96.

Goldstein, H., (1979), 'Improving policing: A problem-oriented approach', *Crime and Delinquency,* 25, pp. 236—58.

Goodgame, D. T., and Rao, Y. V., *An Analysis and Definition of Basic Training Requirements for Municipal Police Officers in Texas,* Occupational Research Program, Texas A & M University.

Gourley, G. D., (1954), 'Police-public relations', *Annals,* 291, p. 136.

Greenberg, B., (1976), *Felony Investigation Decision Model,* Stanford Research Institute, Menlo Park, Calif.

Greenberg, D., Kessler, R., and Logan, C., (1978), 'Crime Rates and Arrest Rates: A Causal Analysis', unpublished paper.

Greenwood, P., Chaiken, J., and Petersilia, J., (1977), *The Criminal Investigation Process,* D. C. Heath, Lexington, Mass.

Greenwood, P., and Petersilia, J., (1975), *The Criminal Investigation Process, vol. I, Summary and Policy Implications,* National Institute of Law Enforcement and Criminal Justice (Rand Corporation), US Government Printing Office, Washington, DC.

Greenwood, M. J., and Wadycki, (1973), 'Crime rates and public expenditures for police protection: their interaction', *Review of Social Economy,* 31, pp. 138—51.

Guyot, D., (1977), 'Instrument for Survey of Public Attitudes in Newark, New Jersey, unpublished.

Heller, N., and McEwan, T., (1973), 'Applications of crime seriousness information in police departments', *Journal of Criminal Justice,* 1, pp. 241-53.

Hindelang, M. J., (1976), *Criminal Victimisation in Eight American Cities,* Ballinger Publishing Company, Cambridge, Mass.

Houston Police Department (1976), *Task Inventory for Sworn Class A Positions: Validation of Selection and Promotion Procedures Study.*

Jones, E. T., (1973), 'Evaluating everyday policies: police activity and crime incidence', *Urban Affairs Quarterly,* 8, pp. 267—79.

Kelling, G. L., Pate, T., Dieckman, D., and Brown, C. E., (1974) *The Kansas City Patrol Experiment: A Technical Report,* Police Coundation, Washington, DC.

Kelling, G. L., (1978), 'The quality of urban life and the police', in Conrad, J. P., (ed.), *The Evolution of Criminal Justice: A Guide for Practical Criminologists,* Sage Publications, Beverly Hills, Calif.

Kelling, G. L., and Fogel, D., (1978), 'Police patrol—some future directions', in Cohn, W., (ed.), *The Future of Policing,* Sage Publications, Beverly Hills, Calif.

Kelling, G. L., and Wycoff, M. A., (1978), *The Dallas Experience: Organisational Reform,* Police Foundation, Washington, DC.

Krajick, K., (1978), 'Does patrol prevent crime?' *Police Magazine,* September.

Larson, R. C., Colton, K. W., and Larson, G. C., (1978), 'Evaluation of a Phase I implementation of an Automatic Vehicle Monitoring (AVM) system in St Louis', in Colton, K. W., (ed.), *Police Computer Technology,* D. C. Heath, Lexington, Mass.

Levine, J. P., (1975), 'The ineffectiveness of adding police to prevent crime', *Public Policy,* 23, pp. 523—45.

Logan, C. H., (1975), 'Arrest rates and deterrence', *Social Science Quarterly,* December, pp. 376—89.

McPheters, L., and Stronge, W., (1974), 'Law enforcement expenditures and urban crime', *National Tax Journal,* 27, pp. 633—43.

Marx, G. T., and Archer, D., (1972), *Community Police Patrols: An Exploratory Inquiry,* National Technical Information Service, Springfield, Va.

Mehay, S. L., (1974), *The Production of Crime Deterrence by Urban Police Departments,* Sir George Williams Faculty Working Paper, 1974—23.

Mehay, S. L., and Furlong, W. J., (1978), *The Deterrent Effect of Urban Police Activities: Theoretical Approaches and Empirical Evidence for Canadian Cities,* Solicitor General of Canada, Ottawa, Ont.

Miller, J., and Fry, L., (1976), 'Re-examining assumptions about education and professionalism in law enforcement', *Journal of Police Science and Administration,* 4, pp. 187—96.

Morris, D., and Tweeten, L., (1971), 'The cost of controlling crime: a study in economics of city life', *Annals of Regional Science,* 5, pp. 33—49.

Municipal Performance Report, (1973), *City Crime,* New York Council on Municipal Performance, May-June.

Myren, R. A., (1972), 'Decentralisation and citizen participation in criminal justice systems', *Public Administration Review,* 32, pp.

718—38.

O'Connor, R. J., and Gilman, B., (1978), 'The police role in deterring crime', in Cramer, J. A., (ed.), *Preventing Crime,* Sage Publications, Beverly Hills, Calif.

Ostrom, E., (1976), 'Police Consolidation and Economics of Scale: Do they go Together?: T-16 series by the Workshop in Political Theory and Policy Analysis, April.

Ostrom, E., (1979), 'Workshop in Political Theory and Policy Analysis'.

Ostrom, E., Parks, R. B., and Whitaker, G., (1976), 'A Public Service Industry Approach to the Study of Police in Metropolitan Areas', Police Services Study, Technical Report, T-19.

Pate, T., Bowers, B. A., and Parks, R., (1976), *Three Approaches to Criminal Apprehension in Kansas City: An Evaluation Report,* Police Foundation, Washington, DC.

Pate, T., Ferrera, A., Bowers, R. A., and Lorence, J., (1976), *Police Response Time,* Police Foundation, Washington, DC.

Phillips, L. H., and Howell, J., (1976), 'Handguns and homicide: minimizing losses and the costs of control', *Journal of Legal Studies,* 5, pp. 463—78.

Pogue, T., (1975), 'Effect of police expenditures on crime rates: some evidence', *Public Finance Quarterly,* 3, pp. 14—44.

Police Foundation, (1972), *Kansas City Citizen Survey,* Police Foundation, Washington, DC, unpublished.

Police Foundation, (1977), *Instrument for Survey of Robbery Victims and Witnesses in Birmingham,* Police Foundation, Washington, DC, unpublished.

Regoli, R. M., (1976), 'The effects of college education on the maintenance of police cynicism', *Journal of Police Science and Administration,* 4, pp. 340—5.

Reppetto, T. A., (1975), 'The influence of police organisational style on crime control effectiveness', *Journal of Police Science and Administration,* 3, pp. 274—9.

Rosenfeld, M., and Thornton, R. F., (1976), *The Development and Validation of a Multi-Jurisdictional Police Examination,* Center for Occupational and Professional Assessment, Educational Testing Service, Princeton, New Jersey.

Schack, S., (1977), *Improving Patrol Productivity, vol. II, Specialized Patrol,* US Government Printing Office, Washington, DC.

Schnelle, J. F., Kirchner, R. E., Casey, J. D., Useltor, P. H., and McNees, M. P., (1977), 'Patrol evaluation research: a multiple baseline analysis of police patrol during day and night hours', *Journal of Applied Behaviour Analysis,* 10, pp. 33—40.

Schwartz, A. L., and Clarren, S. N., (1977), *The Cincinnati Team*

Policing Experiment: A Summary Report, Police Foundation, Washington, DC.

Schwartz, A. L., and Clarren, S. N., (1978), *The Cincinnati Team Policing Experiment: A Technical Report,* Police Foundation, Washington, DC.

Skogan, W., (1974), 'The validity of official crime statistics: an empirical investigation', *Social Science Quarterly,* 55, pp. 25—38.

Skogan, W. G., (1976), 'Crime and crime rates', in Skogan, W. G., (ed.), *Sample Surveys of Victims of Crimes,* Ballinger, Cambridge, Mass.

Sherman, L. W., Milton, C. H., and Kelly, T. V., (1973), *Team Policing: Seven Case Studies,* Police Foundation, Washington, DC.

Smith, D. C., and Ostrom, E., (1973), 'The Effects of Training and Education on Police Attitudes and Performance: A Preliminary Analysis', Workshop in Political Theory and Policy Analysis, Bloomington, Indiana.

Swimmer, G., (1974), 'The relationship of police and crime', *Criminology,* 12, pp. 293—314.

Swimmer, F., (1974), 'Measurement of the effectiveness of urban law enforcement: a simultaneous approach', *Southern Economic Journal,* 40, pp. 618—30.

Thaler, R., (1977), 'An econometric analysis of property crime', *Journal of Public Economics,* 8, pp. 37—51.

Tien, J. M., Simon, J. W., and Larson, R. C., (1978), *The Wilmington Split-Force Experiment,* National Institute of Law Enforcement and Criminal Justice, Law Enforcement Assistance Administration, Washington, DC.

Votey, H., and Phillips, L., (1975), 'Crime control in California', *Journal of Legal Studies,* 4.

Ward, R. H., Ward, T. J., and Feeley, J., (1975), *Police Robbery Control Manual,* Law Enforcement Assistance Administration, Washington, DC.

Washnis, G. J., (1976), *Citizen Involvement in Crime Prevention,* Lexington Books, Lexington, Mass.

Waskow, A. I., (1976), 'Community control of the police', *Trans-Action,* 7, pp. 4—7.

Wasson, D. K., (1975), *Community Based Preventive Policing: A Review,* John D. Crawford & Co. Ltd., Toronto, Ont.

Webb, K. W., et al., (1977a), *Specialized Patrol Projects,* Law Enforcement Assistance Administration, Washington, DC.

Webb, K. W., et al., (1977b), *Assessment of the Knowledge on on Specialized Patrol,* Institute for Human Resources Research, Bethesda, Md.

Weirman, C. M., (1978), 'Variances of ability measurement scores obtained by college and non-college educated troopers, *Police Chief*, 40.

Wellford, C., (1975), 'Crime and the police: A multivariate analysis', *Criminology*, 12, pp. 195—223.

Wilson, J. Q., (1968), *Varieties of Police Behavior: The Management of Law and Order in Eight Communities*, Harvard University Press, Cambridge, Mass.

Wilson, J. Q., and Boland, B., (1978), 'The effect of police on crime rates', *Law and Society Review*, 12, pp. 367—90.

Woollack, S., and associates, *The Validation of Entry-Level Police Officer Selection Procedures in the State of Washington*.

Wycoff, M. A., and Susmilch, C. E., (1978), 'The Relevance of College Education for Policing: Continuing the Dialogue', paper presented to the Annual Meeting of the American Society of Criminology, Dallas, Tex., November.

Zimring, F. E., (1978), 'Police experiments in general deterrence', in Blumstein, J., Cohen, J., and Nagin, D., (eds.), *Deterrence and Incapacitation Estimating the Effects of Criminal Sanctions on Crime Rates*, National Academy of Sciences, Washington, DC.

5 Police effectiveness and the public: the limitations of official crime rates
A. K. Bottomley and C. A. Coleman

> The average citizen thinks of the police as an organisation primarily concerned with preventing crime and catching criminals. When crime increases or criminals go uncaught, the conventional public response is to demand more or better policemen. When the crime rate goes down or a particularly heinous crime is solved, the police often get— or at least try to take—the credit. (Wilson, 1975, p. 81)

This quotation from James Q. Wilson's essay on 'The Police and Crime' in his provocative book, *Thinking about Crime,* aptly reflects the dilemmas of both the police and the public in the face of apparently ever-increasing crime rates in contemporary urban societies. As far as the general public is concerned there is an urgent demand for an answer to the problems of crime control and 'law and order', and more often than not this answer is sought at the direct, practical level of law enforcement represented by the police. The police, despite the fact that much of their everyday activity is unconnected with crime, become pressured from different directions into accepting a definition of their role that is primarily focused upon crime and almost unwittingly are drawn into a web of collusion that equates police effectiveness in a community with a decreasing or at least stabilised level of crime. At a time when, in Britain, renewed attention is being paid by social scientists to the work of the police, including for the first time to ways in which their effectiveness can be appropriately evaluated (see Clarke and Heal, 1979), it is important to question some of the underlying assumptions. In particular a close look needs to be taken at what are perceived as the primary *aims* of policing, and, in the research context, at the validity of the *criteria* used to measure any changes that may occur in police effectiveness. Inasmuch as official criminal statistics are frequently used for the purposes of evaluation this paper will address itself to the inherent limitations of utilising existing statistics in this way, whether of reported and recorded crimes, or the 'clear-up' rates of so-called 'detected' crimes. Research findings from some recent British studies relevant to understanding the processes of the construction and interpretation of crime rates will be examined, and consideration given to the implications for those embarking upon research in this important area.

It ought to be made clear at the outset that although the police 'effectiveness' that is being discussed here relates exclusively to police crime work, we do not wish this to be taken as a sign that we accept the distorted public image of the crime-centred nature of the police role. However, insofar as this emerging field of study is inextricably bound up with public expectations in their socio-political context, at both local and national level, the comments that we offer are located within the conventional frame of reference but seek to open up the debate about the nature and scope of the police role in society. ——

Most attempts to analyse the effectiveness of police crime work have started from the two traditional aims of modern police systems, namely the *prevention* and *detection* of crime. The ease with which these terms slip off the tongues of police administrators and community liaison officers conceals not only the complexity of what each entails but also the meanings that are often attached to them by uninitiated audiences. So often 'crime prevention' in the police-community context refers to local campaigns to encourage householders or car owners to ensure the security of their property, or perhaps to the provision of extra leisure facilities for unattached young people on a bleak housing estate; similarly, the 'detection' of crime may be subject to a variety of interpretations, ranging from what should strictly be called the discovery of crime, to the assumed methods of police suspicion and investigation that ultimately lead to bringing offenders to book. For the researcher, however, and the majority of experienced police officers, these twin aims carry more precise meanings, at once narrower and yet with potentially wider implications than implied by the common public misconceptions.

Crime prevention signifies those police activities that are intended to reduce the amount of crime committed in the community, 'in advance' as it were—as opposed to any reduction of crime that might result from known offenders being 'taken out of circulation', by arrest and subsequent custodial sentence. So although this includes police advice to the public as to how they might reduce the risk of victimisation, it is also interpreted more broadly for operational purposes in terms of the *deterrent* aims of police street patrolling and police presence in other crime-prone public (and semi-public) settings. It is this presumed deterrent capacity that has been fundamental to many of the major studies of the effectiveness of police patrol carried out in the United States. To the extent that these studies are seen by those in other countries as providing models for further research it seems important to clarify how central a part the purely deterrent

71

objective plays within the overall crime prevention role of the police, and whether or not other objectives ought to receive equal (or greater) attention from researchers, such as the practical police roles in reducing opportunities for crime commission, both in the conventional sense of encouraging primary security precautions to protect persons and property, and more positively in the provision of opportunities and facilities that might divert potential offenders from future careers in crime. However, whatever priority is given to the variety of possible objectives and techniques of crime prevention, the usual measure of success is the amount of reported crime in the community concerned, and it is the validity of this criterion that we will examine first, after some preliminary remarks on other possible objectives of police crime work.

Crime detection relates in a more direct and immediate way to what is seen by many police and members of the public as the central task of contemporary policing. It does not mean here the initial discovery of crimes for which, as we shall see below, the police rely very heavily on the victims and witnesses directly involved, but rather the discovery and apprehension of those responsible so that known crimes may be regarded by the police as 'cleared-up' and the identity of the offenders established to their satisfaction. The processes of police investigation and detection have been the subject of several important research studies in America. Many myths deriving from a persuasive diet of 'detective' fiction in the various media are now gradually being dispelled, but it is proving far more difficult to know how to fill the gap created. It is not enough to show how little classic 'detection' work goes into the successful 'solving' of crimes known to the police, or how unrealiable the officially constructed 'clear-up' rates are as measures of police efficiency. There is a need for a more honest appraisal of the realities of the problems of crime detection facing the police, and greater openness between the police, the public and the politicians in working towards the possibility of more meaningful criteria (if any such exist) relating to the satisfactory apprehension of offenders.

Finally, before embarking upon a closer examination of the validity of statistics of reported crime and the clear-up rates, a third possible objective must be introduced. For members of the general public the concept and reality of 'police effectiveness' is inevitably somewhat intangible and subjective, with their perception of it depending on a mixture of 'mass-mediated' statistics and selectively reported crime incidents and trials, together with first or second-hand knowledge of crime in the community. Paradoxically, also, the more well-informed a citizen becomes about the 'official' facts of crime in his locality the more confused and uncertain will be his knowledge of how effective the police are in the prevention and detection of crime. In this situation of shared doubt as to the achievements of what are regarded as primary police objectives in the field of crime control, it may often happen that a secondary 'strategy' comes to be adopted by the police, that of *public reassurance*. By this, we do not mean the instrumental type of 'community service' mentioned by Wilson, of which the objective is to enable crime work to be more effective by the community becoming more co-operative in assisting the police and providing criminal intelligence (Wilson, 1975, pp. 90—1). On the contrary, public reassurance and citizen satisfaction with the way the police handle complaints and follow up cases can be seen as an end in itself, and one which has often ranked high in surveys of public opinion on the police (e.g., Bordua and Tifft, 1971; Furstenberg and Wellford, 1973). Furthermore in certain fashionable areas of operational police work, such as 'response time analysis', even if no hard evidence emerges that fast response leads to more arrests, it may still be possible to argue in its favour if it increases public perception of efficiency on the part of the police. At the end of the day we may agree with Skogan:

> ... for most kinds of crime, police work provides largely symbolic satisfactions. In the light of low clearance rates and soaring crime rates, the primary function of the police at the individual level is to 'cool the mark out', assisting citizens in coming to terms with their new status as victims ... At the community level, convincing voters and opinion leaders that 'something is being done' is perhaps the most important pay-off of patrolling. (Skogan, 1975, p. 50).

Crime prevention and recorded crime rates

Most of the early studies of the effectiveness of police patrol in the prevention of crime relied upon changes in the officially recorded statistics of 'crimes known to the police' as their basic measure of success. The Kansas City Preventive Patrol experiment was the first major study to incorporate a much wider range of criteria, by using community social surveys of public attitudes and experiences of crime victimisation (see Kelling, et al., 1974). In view of the considerable extra demand upon resources of time and effort required to mount adequate surveys of this kind it seems important to underline the serious limitations of reliance upon official crime rates in police effectiveness research. Furthermore, by attempting to locate the precise points at which 'distortion' may occur it should be possible to assess the potential value of alternative measures, whether victimisation studies or more careful monitoring of the various stages in the process of producing official statistics. There are many quite obvious and by now generally well known pitfalls in the assumption that the reporting of crime by members of the public (whether as victims, witnesses, etc.) follows any predictable trends, but there are also some less obvious and less publicised ways in which police policy and practices in dealing with crime complaints can have a significant influence upon the pattern of recorded crime rates.

There are at least four different elements in the construction and interpretation of recorded crime rates that need to be emphasised:

1 The *discovery* of crime: the vast majority of crimes that make up the total officially recorded by the police are discovered and reported to them by members of the public, and do not become known as a result of direct police initiative.

2 The *reporting* of crime by victims and witnesses is related to a wide variety of factors including public perception of the effectiveness of the police and their accessibility in the local community.

3 The *recording* of crime by the police is a complex and variable sifting process that may result in a large drop-out rate in the stage between citizens' crime complaints and the records compiled by the police for official purposes.

4 The *classification* of crimes by the police is also subject to variations and discretionary decision-making that may significantly affect the pattern of crime that emerges.

Each of these elements will be examined briefly with supporting evidence drawn mainly from our own research and that of other researchers currently working in this field in Britain (see Bottomley and Coleman, 1976, in press; Sparks, et al., 1977; McCabe and Sutcliffe, 1978; Mawby, 1979). Throughout this discussion, with its primary focus on the prospects and problems of research into police effectiveness, it will be useful to keep in mind the relative roles of the public and the police, so as to be aware of those elements in the situation that are within the discretionary control of the police themselves and thus more likely to be affected (whether consciously or otherwise) by their appreciation of the context and consequences of particular procedures and policies.

Discovery of crime

Our study of a sample of more than 2,800 crime complaints initially reported to the police of a medium sized city in the North of England during 1972 showed that of the 2,500 finally recorded

Table 5.1

Mode of discovery, according to type of offence
(in percentages, $n = 2,506$)

Offence group	Police		Non-police				
	Direct (n=142)	Indirect (n=203)	Victim (personal) (n=1,427)	Victim (organisation) (n=570)	Member of public (n=82)	Other (n=46)	Not known (n=36)
Violence against the person (n=103)	5	—	90	—	1	3	1
Sexual offences (n=26)	4	4	69	—	4	12	8
Burglary and robbery (n=776)	5	4	61	22	6	1	2
Theft and handling (n=1,473)	6	10	56	23	2	2	3
Fraud and forgery (n=75)	4	37	7	44	1	4	3
Criminal damage (n=53)	11	—	25	51	11	2	—

as crimes the police were responsible directly or indirectly for the discovery of only 14 per cent, and the majority of these (59 per cent) came to light indirectly during investigations by the CID (see Table 5.1). Confirmation of the relatively minor police role in the early stages of the discovery of crime is provided from another British study, carried out by Rob Mawby in Sheffield, in which an identical proportion (14 per cent) of crimes was discovered by the police, of which more than six out of every ten were discovered indirectly (Mawby, 1979). Similar studies in the United States, although based on slightly different offence samples, have revealed comparable patterns; for example, in Black's study of police-citizen encounters in Boston, Chicago and Washington, out of a total of 5,713 observed incidents only 13 per cent arose from police initiative (Black, 1970, 1971), and in the earlier analysis of discovery in juvenile cases by Sellin and Wolfgang (1964) in the more serious offences the police discovered the initial event in just 16 per cent of all cases.

This means that in the vast majority of cases the initiative in whether or not to make a crime known to the authorities lies with individuals other than the police. More often than not this is the direct victim, or someone acting on the victim's behalf (e.g., a close relative, or an employee of an organisation that has suffered criminal loss or injury). Within the large group of those indirectly related to the victim or victimised organisation are those who have a specific responsibility for looking after property, ranging from the school caretaker and the factory night watchman to the store detectives employed in most of the larger department stores. The decisions of these key personnel, relating to the reporting of offences, has long been a neglected area by researchers which needs remedying if a comprehensive understanding of crime statistics is wanted. For certain offences their role is absolutely central; shoplifting is the most obvious example, where the work of store detectives can have a tremendous influence upon statistics of reported theft, particularly in city centres, and make literal nonsense of clear-up rates. Almost half (47 per cent) of the 221 recorded shoplifting offences in our sample were directly discovered by store detectives, who were also indirectly involved in most of the 53 offences (24 per cent) admitted during police questioning; thus, store detectives played a major part in the discovery of almost three-quarters of the shoplifting offences that appeared in the official records, amounting in fact to more than *the total of all crimes* discovered by direct police activity. In other publicly sensitive offences also, such as vandalism and school thefts/ burglaries, the role of such personnel can be crucial, and, unless carefully taken into account, changes in the policy and practices of these 'private law enforcers' (to borrow Mawby's phrase for them) can undermine completely the validity of attempts to monitor the effects of changes in police policy upon specific crime rates.

Finally, we found that in only 3 per cent of the total were crimes reported to the police by members of the public who were neither directly nor indirectly the victims. These included mainly neighbours, workmates, or casual passers by, and varied according to the type of offence. It may be that certain forms of police-community campaigns or related research projects could have a significant effect upon the role of such members of the public in taking more positive steps to combat an apparent reluctance to get involved (see also Conklin and Bittner, 1973).

The clear message that emerges from research into how crimes are discovered is that the police have relatively little control of their initial 'input' as far as most indictable crimes are concerned. There are, of course, the 14 or 15 per cent of crimes currently discovered, directly or indirectly, by police work that could in theory be influenced by changes in policing, especially perhaps in the way CID officers bring to light previously undiscovered offences during investigations and questioning of suspects; there are also certain other offences, generally of a more minor nature, that are directly responsive to changes in 'proactive' policing, that tend to have been over-emphasised in the past but ought not for that reason to be completely overlooked.

Reporting of crime

Having established that the general public play a major part in the initial discovery of crime it is natural to refer next to the comparatively large amount of research conducted during the last few decades into the nature and extent of the 'dark figure' of unreported crime. The general findings of this research are now well known and recent studies in Britain have confirmed what has been shown elsewhere (see West and Farrington, 1973; Belson, 1975; Sparks, et al., 1977). For example, the study of victimisation in the three London boroughs of Brixton, Hackney and Kensington in 1972, carried out by Richard Sparks and his colleagues, reached the startling conclusion that:

> ... if our survey based estimates are accepted as showing the amounts of indictable crime against individual victims in the three areas in 1972, then less than *one-tenth* of those crimes covered by our survey which could have been recorded in the police statistics in our areas in 1972 were actually recorded there. For offences against the person and miscellaneous thefts the proportion is only about two to four per cent. Even for

burglary and thefts in dwelling houses, the figure is only about 24 per cent. (Sparks, et al., 1977, p. 153)

It is findings such as these which help to fuel the common scepticism of official criminal statistics, increasingly shared by academic criminologists, law enforcement practitioners and members of the public alike. In the face of the cumulative research evidence it would indeed be a brave (or foolish) man who attempts seriously to defend the use of such statistics in the kind of precise way needed to test assumptions of deterrent effectiveness implicit in police research. It is of course perfectly possible to argue, like some of the early nineteenth century statisticians of crime, that some significance can indeed be attached to changes in the recorded crime rates, without implying anything about the absolute relationship between recorded and unrecorded crime. To counter that sort of argument, in the context of the present debate, it would be useful to be able to cite evidence suggesting that in certain circumstances the inclination of victims and witnesses to report crimes may be affected by their attitudes towards and expectations of the police, so that changes in respect of the latter might be expected to result in changes in crime reporting behaviour. There is certainly plenty of evidence from victim opinion surveys that one of the main reasons for non-reporting is a lack of confidence in the police ability to do anything effective or useful to help. In Sparks' survey the most common reason given for not reporting incidents was a belief that it was 'not sufficiently serious', but the second commonest reason was that the police would be unable to do anything useful about the matter; it seemed, however, that 'these responses related mainly to the facts of the particular incident, rather than to a general belief that the police were incompetent' (Sparks, et al., 1977, p. 124).

Space does not permit this line of argument to be pursued much further here, save simply to re-emphasise that where circumstances dictate the use of official statistics as the only criterion for purposes of evaluation it is vital to take account of changes in reporting behaviour that might flow indirectly from changes in the way a community is policed; these changes may lead either to more or less reporting, but in any case need to be separated from intended effects upon the commission of crime itself. To give an example of a rather different kind, there is evidence from places as far apart as Uganda, East Africa, and Nashville, Tennessee, that changes in the physical accessibility of the local police, whether in terms of the location of police stations or a change from foot patrol to 'panda' cars, are likely to have an effect on the threshold of incidents that people are likely to consider worth reporting to the police (Tanner, 1970; Schnelle, et al., 1975).

In contrast with the apparent lack of scope for the exercise of police discretion in the discovery of crime, it is becoming increasingly clear that this lack of scope in the earliest stages leading to the eventual production of official crime rates may be more than compensated by the discretionary practices apparent in the sifting of crime complaints by the police organisation before being finally recorded as crimes for official purposes. Although the details and terminology of these processes may differ from country to country, and even from one police force to another, the essential features appear the same, and raise equally problematic issues for the interpretation of any figures that are produced by the police, especially when they are aware of the political significance of the outcome.

In his classic study of policing in the United States Skolnick claimed that about 20 per cent of original crime reports never found their way into official crime statistics because of the variable ways in which different city forces regarded certain crime complaints as 'unfounded' or merely as 'suspicious circumstances' for later follow-up by detectives (Skolnick, 1966, pp. 164–81; for dramatic illustration of the wider political aspects of these practices in America see Center and Smith, 1973; Seidman and Couzens, 1974; Conklin, 1975).

In England, John Lambert collected similar statistics of 'no crimes' (as they are usually called in this country) for a Birmingham police division during a four-month period in 1967: out of a total of 2,003 indictable property 'crimes' reported to the police, 93 (5 per cent) were eventually written off as 'no crimes' (Lambert, 1970, p. 43). We saw this as an important part of our survey in the Northern city and Table 5.2 shows that as many as 11 per cent of the initial crime reports were written off by the police as 'no crimes'. Cycle thefts featured largely, as 30 per cent of initially reported thefts were written off as 'no crimes' when the cycles were recovered by their owners undamaged within a day or two; but even excluding these, almost one-fifth of reported criminal damage incidents resulted in 'no crimes', as did one in six of reported offences of violence against the person and more than one in ten sexual offences. A more detailed analysis of the circumstances in which the police reached their 'no crime' decisions in cases other than those involving cycles, revealed that 35 per cent were written off by the police exercising their discretion in the interpretation of the surrounding circumstances; in 19 per cent of the cases it transpired that literally 'no crime' had been committed (e.g., 'lost' property turned up); in 15 per cent of the cases the victim did not wish to prosecute (including more than 60 per cent of the 'no crimes' in cases of personal violence); and

Table 5.2
Initial crime reports and 'no crimes'

Offence group	Initial crime reports	Subsequently classified as 'no crimes'	
	No.	No.	%
Violence against the person	124	21	17
Sexual offences	28	3	11
Burglary and robbery	834	53	6
Theft and handling (exc. cycle theft)	1,332	109	8
Cycle theft	350	106	30
Fraud and forgery	81	6	7
Criminal damage	67	13	19
Other offences	3	2	67
Total	2,819	313	11

other less common reasons included cases where the complainant discovered new information in the light of which the complaint was withdrawn, or where there did not seem to the police to be enough evidence to prosecute, or where there was a complicated domestic situation (for further details see Coleman and Bottomley, 1976; Bottomley and Coleman, in press).

In view of the numerous ambiguities and inconsistencies we found surrounding the procedures and policies for writing off crime reports as 'no crime', it came as no surprise that national figures confirm the existence of disparities. Statistics for all the metropolitan and non-metropolitan police forces in England and Wales for 1977 (excluding London) show that there was a variation in the proportions of initial crime reports that were regarded as no-crime incidents, ranging from less than 1 per cent to more than 8 per cent (CIPFA, 1978, Table 9). Although there was some tendency for high 'no crime' rates to occur in forces which had a higher than average clear-up rate—suggesting a plausible connection between the two—this general association occurred mainly because all the large metropolitan forces (with low clear-up) had 'no crime' rates of less than 3 per cent, and, in fact, of the half dozen forces with the highest clear-up rates two had 'no crime' rates of 7 per cent or more, but two had the lowest rates of 1 per cent or less!

An important recently published study in Britain has documented the nature of such disparities between two police forces. McCabe and Sutcliffe (1978) compared the ways in which the police dealt with reported crime incidents and other complaints or requests for police action from members of the public in Oxford and Salford. In Oxford, during 1974, out of 10,116 crimes known to the police 617 (6 per cent) were written off as 'no crimes'; whereas in Salford, during a similar 12-month period, out of 12,994 crimes known to the police only 205 (less than 2 per cent) were written off. Different offences featured in the 'no crime' category of these two cities, but the same sorts of police reasoning were associated with the decisions as those found in our study. However, a major conclusion of the McCabe and Sutcliffe research was that significant differences in the 'no crime' rates for different police forces could be due largely to different policies and procedures in the earlier stages *before the writing of official crime reports:*

> Clearly the initial write-off within each month will depend to some extent upon the recording policy and practice in the area. Where crime reports are filed only after a fairly full investigation, the 'no-crime' rate should be low. But this cannot account for all the variation between one police area and another. (McCabe and Sutcliffe, 1978, p. 73)

In reported assaults and burglaries the Salford police wrote crime reports more frequently than at Oxford, and the authors suggested that this could be due not only to differences in the type of offences reported but also to the different ways in which cases were allocated between the uniformed and detective branches:

> Certainly the Salford police, as we observed them, worked under great pressure and it may be that, in certain circumstances, an arrest or the reporting of an offence and immediate transfer to the CID is a quicker, more economic solution to the citizen's complaint than discussion, explanation, or advice. (McCabe and Sutcliffe, 1978, p. 56)

Sparks' victimisation research team, despite the different basis of their study, also revealed an apparently large discrepancy between the number of incidents reported to the police in the London boroughs surveyed and the number appearing in police records; so that in addition to the very large number of *unreported* crimes, possibly as many as two-thirds of what were reported as 'crimes' by the public were not finally recorded as such by the police, with 'under-recording' being especially common in cases of alleged assault and thefts from the person (Sparks, et al., 1977, pp. 155–8). There exists considerable supporting evidence for similar practices in America. Biderman's

Columbia survey for the President's Commission in 1967 showed that less than half of all reported incidents were classified as crime by the police (Biderman, 1967); Black reported that an official crime report was written in less than two out of every three cases in his sample of police–complainant encounters (Black, 1970); and Pepinsky emphasised the importance of the initial message from the despatcher in his study of Minneapolis patrolmen, who filed an official report in a minority of reported 'crime' incidents (Pepinsky, 1976).

It would be convenient for research on police effectiveness if crime rates could be regarded as measuring crime rather in the way that a thermometer measures temperature. The evidence presented here indicates to the contrary, because not only does the public have a considerable impact on the 'input' to police work, but the way in which the police process that input is subject to a variety of variables, the interaction of which is only just beginning to be understood. (Manning's chapter in this volume is an important contribution to this understanding.) Naturally, also, the police will have more than a passing interest in what is defined as crime for official purposes since the crime rate, and its derivative the clear-up rate, are taken by the public and politicians as *the* indicator of the problems faced by the police, and their effectiveness in dealing with those problems.

Classification of crimes

The final element to which we want to draw attention is the way in which police decisions affect the classification of recorded crimes. Other commentators have emphasised the influence that police recording practices may have on official statistics, making qualitative comparisons between different periods virtually impossible. Traditionally quoted examples in Britain include the abolition of the 'suspected stolen' book in the Metropolitan Police District in 1931, the retention by the police (since 1950) of the original classification of the reported crime in all cases except homicide (rather than amending it in the light of further investigation, reduced charges, or court verdicts—see the effect on crimes of violence reported by McClintock, et al., 1963), and recent changes in the instructions to the police about the recording of minor thefts and criminal damage under certain values. Most of these changes came about as a result of official instructions to the police to change their procedures, and although we are not aware that any such allegations have been made publicly in Britain, the inherent potential for political manipulation, at the national or local level, is very great indeed, as the American experience during and prior to the Nixon administration testifies (see

Seidman and Couzens, 1974; Morrisey, 1972).

Part of the problem lies in the fact that the legal and statistical categories used for official purposes have a vagueness and ambiguity that renders them open to misunderstanding on the part of the general public and allows a measure of flexibility to the police in allocating a particular incident to an official category. The situational classifications developed at the Cambridge Institute of Criminology would go some way towards clarifying the meaning to be attached to certain categories, especially in crimes of violence (see McClintock and Gibson, 1961; McClintock, et al., 1963); but despite the recommendations of the Perks Committee in 1967 little progress has been made in introducing such refinements in routine statistics, although the annual Report of the Commissioner of the London Metropolitan Police provides a useful classification of robbery and draws a distinction between 'forcible entry' and 'walk-in' burglaries.

To give a small example of the sort of issues that are involved, a feature that we found particularly important in interpreting the local statistics of burglaries in dwelling houses was the number of cases in which *prepayment meters only were attacked:* 170 (37 per cent) of the 454 recorded cases of burglary in dwellings were of this kind, with no other property in the house stolen or damaged, and yet as far as the public was concerned they were all included within the sensitive category of 'house burglary' in the Chief Constable's annual report. From the police accounts that we studied the decision as to whether to classify an incident of meter theft as house burglary or simply 'theft meter' emerged as a particularly interesting illustration of the operation of the 'practical reasoning' of the police in which their assessment of the 'moral character' of the complainant was crucial (see Coleman and Bottomley, 1976).

We reject the simplistic view that there is necessarily a 'right' or 'wrong' way for the police to classify any specific incident, but favour an approach that starts from a realistic appreciation of the working situation of investigating officers and attempts to discover and compare the customary methods of resolving any problems or ambiguities that may arise (for an opposite set of assumptions see Ferracuti, et al., 1962; rather less judgemental is Littrell, 1973). Police crime classification decisions are rarely simple or straightforward; they are very much dependent on the knowledge of the context of the events in question, the complainant and suspects and the officer's evaluation of and interaction with them. If additional constraints are present, in the shape of administrative manipulation of crime rates, or unfamiliar pressure of a research project that is monitoring police work, modifications can be expected to occur in the application of traditional 'practical reasoning' that may well lead to an outcome in official statistical terms that is different from what it might otherwise have been.

Crime detection, investigation and clear-up rates

The official record of the percentage of crimes 'cleared-up' by the police (commonly referred to as the 'detection rate') tends to be the statistic that is used by the mass media, by politicians and even by police administrators (who perhaps ought to know better!) as a measure of police effectiveness in the 'war against crime'. Since the clear-up rate is frequently the *only* easily quantifiable and publicly available measure that seems to allow comparisons from year to year and between different forces, it frequently becomes taken as the measure of 'output' or 'productivity' in the performance of the police task. This tendency perpetuates and feeds the myth that police work can be equated with crime work and that the police spend most of their time 'catching criminals'. Public conceptions about how this is achieved are also probably largely mythical.

Research studies attempting to evaluate the effectiveness of different methods of crime investigation also frequently use the clear-up rate as the measure of effectiveness (see for example Elliott, 1978). It therefore seems important to clarify certain aspects of its interpretation and ultimate significance in relation to police work in the investigation of crime and the detection of offenders.

An alternative measure of police effectiveness in dealing with crime is the arrest rate: arrests are commonly used as a major criterion of formal and informal intra-organisational evaluation of the performance of individual police officers. It must be stressed that arrest rates and clear-up rates cannot be regarded as reflecting, even roughly, the same thing. The fundamental points are that offences can be cleared by other techniques than arrest and that arrests do not necessarily lead to clearances. Indeed Greenwood and his colleagues found that if police departments were ranked by region according to arrest rates and then by clearance rates, the rankings in one case were almost exactly the reverse of the rankings in the other, causing them to comment:

> This observation clearly illustrates the futility of attempting to use either arrest rates or clearance rates as measures of performance for comparing police departments. Evidently it is impossible that departments located in the South Central portion of the United States are at the same time the best in the country and the worst in the country, but interpreting arrest and clearance rates as performance measures appears to lead to this conclusion. (Greenwood et al. 1977, p.84)

Whether the measure of performance used is arrest rate, clear-up rate or any other single unidimensional criterion, our fundamental argument is that any such exercise runs the risk of prejudging the issue of what are or should be the primary aims of policing. Even if it is agreed that police work is appropriately evaluated in terms of its success in the detection of crime, we would argue that clear-up rates as they are presently constructed are inappropriate for that purpose. Regional variations in practices and conditions can make comparisons between the crude clear-up rates of different police departments highly misleading. In addition there are so many different and variable inputs that make a contribution to that magical figure, that it seems unlikely that the activities that go to make up a clear-up rate are best expressed in such a form.

Any researcher who attempts to overcome the problems created by regional differences in practices and conditions by concentrating on a single organisational unit must also be on his guard. Any study attempting to assess the impact of a different method of investigation or organisation upon the clear-up rate must be certain that the other conditions to which that rate is responsive do not vary and therefore contaminate the findings.

Finally, and perhaps most importantly, research has shown that an inordinate emphasis on a single, easily quantifiable performance measure may have unanticipated consequences for police work itself. Officers who are judged mainly on the basis of clear-ups or arrests may be more interested in fulfilling 'production quotas' than about the way in which the job is done. Such an emphasis may lead to a subversion of more abstract, less quantifiable, but perhaps more important goals of police work (Skolnick, 1966). In this section we attempt to illustrate these views by looking at various studies which have examined the production of clear-up rates.

It is well established that the proportion of crimes cleared-up in each offence category varies to a considerable extent. In our own research for example, only 22 per cent of the burglaries and robberies were detected, compared with 79 per cent of the offences of violence against the person and 97 per cent of offences of fraud and forgery. Any attempt to understand figures of this sort must start from a basic appreciation of the significance of the mode of discovery, i.e. the ways in which crimes became known to the police, for the task of detection facing the police. The situation was well summarised by McClintock and Avison in their detailed survey of crime in England and Wales:

Studies on crime detection rates indicate the need for a knowledge of the extent to which the police are faced with genuine problems of detecting unidentified offenders at the time when the offence is reported to them. Such cases have to be contrasted with those crimes that are automatically 'solved' when reported to the police or when the offenders are caught by the police in the course of committing the crime, so that no problem of detection arises. (McClintock and Avison, 1968, p. 109)

In the first place, there are certain whole categories of offence which because of the circumstances surrounding their discovery are cleared-up virtually 'automatically' as soon as they become known to the police: examples range from 'handling stolen goods' and 'theft by employee' to shoplifting and various kinds of frauds, which rarely become known to the police unless the offenders have already been identified, and for which the very high clear-up rate has virtually no significance at all in terms of police effectiveness in *detection*, as such. Shoplifting for example is an offence which gives a considerable boost to clear-up rates, since store detectives and shop workers rarely call in the police unless they have apprehended a suspect. Police are rarely engaged in *detective* work in such cases, although they may well have work to do for the purposes of prosecution. Since the latter is not accurately reflected in clear-up rates, it seems perverse to evaluate police effectiveness in such cases on the basis of those rates.

At the very least, clear-up rates should present separate figures for the 'automatically detected' offences so that some of the grosser mis-interpretations may be avoided. In our own research if all offences of theft and handling had been analysed together, the clear-up rate would have been 45 per cent, but by excluding shoplifting and handling (with a 93 per cent clear-up) it dropped to 34 per cent.

A second point to stress in interpreting different clear-up rates between types of offence is that the extremely high proportion of violence against the person and sexual offences that are detected derives mainly from the large number of such offences in which the victim is closely related to or knows the offender, who is thus immediately identifiable to the police. McClintock and Avison, although suggesting that in some of the most serious crimes the police achieved success because of the high priority assigned to such offences, claimed that the main reason was of a different kind:

In a very high proportion of crimes of violence the crimes were relatively easy to solve because of the association between the offender and victim prior to the offences. In many cases the victim was able to name the offender when reporting the crime to the police, while in cases of murder—especially in the domestic or family situation—there was no doubt as to the identity of the offender ... In respect to murder, sexual offences and crimes of violence, where the attack was made on a stranger and a genuine problem of detection arose, the various detection rates decreased to approximately forty per cent, thus indicating that the police were not outstandingly more successful in detecting these crimes than they were with offences of dishonesty. (McClintock and Avison, 1968, p. 108)

Clearly, therefore, a recognition of the social context in which different crimes are committed and of the personal relationships between victims and offenders must play an essential part in answering the question of whether clear-up rates can be regarded as an index of police performance when it is becoming increasingly clear that many contributory factors in the determination of crime rates are outside their direct control. Interestingly enough, Zander's recent study of cases tried at the Old Bailey found that in 48 per cent of these the defendant had some prior relationship with the victim or someone else giving information about the offence (Zander, 1979).

Finally, when we examine in more detail the processes of investigation and detection, we shall see that it is not only those offences where offender and victim were closely related that produced 'ready made' suspects, but that over a much wider variety of offences the police were presented with few problems of detecting unknown offenders in the classic style of detective fiction. Table 5.3 gives some preliminary results from our own research and shows the ways in which suspects were identified in incidents that were subject to a crime report. It must be stressed that these cases were not necessarily

Table 5.3

Cases with strong initial identifications:
source and type of suspect identification*

Source of identification	Type of identification		Totals
	Detained	named	
Not recorded	1	94	95
Victim/complainant	46	220	266
Police	163	12	175
Store detective	95	8	103
Other	16	59	75
Other offender	0	18	18
Totals	321	411	732

*The 732 cases in this table represent 26 per cent of the total sample of 2,819. Not all the 732 cases ended up as detected or indeed were defined as crimes in the final event.

all subsequently defined as crimes, nor necessarily classified as 'detected' in the final event. We have separated out for analysis cases in which suspects were identified by either being detained at or near the scene of the incident, or were named or pointed out by various agents during initial enquiries.

Most of the cases in the table, especially where a suspect is detained at the scene, present few problems for the police in terms of detection to their satisfaction. These cases are therefore those that are highly likely to be cleared up and that fact will be obvious at an early stage in the process. This does not mean that the job of the police simply ends at this point: suspects (when named rather than detained) must be located (sometimes with difficulty) and the police must often collect further evidence and produce paperwork that will serve for the purposes of prosecution. Indeed the authors of the Rand Corporation study concluded: 'For cases that are solved (i.e., a suspect has been identified), an investigator's average time in post-clearance processing is longer than the time spent in identifying the perpetrator'. (Greenwood, et al., 1977, pp. 229–30) If the same is true in the British context, it seems unfortunate that the proposed measure of effectiveness, i.e. the clear-up rate, is unresponsive to the quantity and quality of those activities.

For present purposes three basic observations can be made about Table 5.3. First, in over a quarter of all incidents subject to a crime report, ready-made suspects were available from or near the outset. Secondly a large proportion of these suspects were provided by members of the public, especially the victim or complainant (266, i.e. 36 per cent) and the store detective (103, i.e. 14 per cent). Thirdly, in those cases where suspects were supplied by being detained by the police, many of these suspects would have been provided by the uniformed branch. It is all to easy to assume from a surface knowledge of police organisation and clear-up rates that detectives from the CID are *the* specialists in crime 'detection'. Chatterton's (1976) work on the relative contribution of both branches to arrest rates is a useful antidote to this view. The important point for present purposes is that cases with ready-made suspects contribute very significantly to clear-up rates and that these initial identifications are often due to characteristics of the crime and its context, and the action taken or information provided by members of the public, all of which are basically beyond the control of the police. Our findings have a close parallel in those of Greenwood, who found that the identity of the offender was available at the time of the reporting of more than half of cases that were eventually cleared-up (Greenwood, et al., 1977, p. 141). Under such conditions it seems unwise to regard the clear-up rate as a simple index of the effectiveness of the police alone in the *investigation* of crime as such.

But what of the remainder of cases, in which no offender is instantly available to the police by means of the mechanisms described above? It might be assumed that it is in this remainder of cases that 'real' detective work is done. This is true, but much over-simplified. A complete answer needs to take into account the administrative procedures used by the police in those situations which may present more intractable problems of detection. It is not commonly realised that official instructions allow a variety of circumstances to count for purposes of 'clearing-up' recorded crimes, apart from the obvious situation of a person being found guilty of the offence in question. These include (a) when a person is charged with the offence, but is subsequently acquitted; (b) when a person has further offences 'taken into consideration' ('TIC') after conviction for another offence; (c) where there is some practical hindrance to prosecution, e.g., if the suspect dies, or if the victim and/or key witnesses are unwilling to give evidence; (d) when a person admits the offence, but is only cautioned by the police, or is under the age of criminal responsibility; and (e) when a person who is already serving a custodial sentence admits to a crime but it is decided that 'no useful purposes would be served by proceeding with the charge' (Home Office, 1971).

Although all of these circumstances raise issues about the interpretation of clear-up rates, it is most important to realise the highly significant contribution which offences 'taken into consideration' can make to those rates. Officially published statistics rarely provide information from which it would be possible to estimate this contribution. For all offence groups combined in our sample, one quarter of cleared-up crimes were achieved by being 'TIC'. There was wide variation in the extent to which different types of offence were cleared up in this manner, so that despite the high clear-up rate in cases of violence and sexual offences, not one was cleared by this method. On the other hand, nearly four out of ten burglaries were cleared in this way. In addition, out of the total of offences cleared by the technique, over half *first became known to the police* when they were admitted by suspects under questioning. Whatever attempts are made to standardise practices within and between police organisations, it would be difficult to control the amount of time and effort spent by officers in achieving clear-ups in this way, thereby producing variations which would make comparisons hazardous.

Other studies indicate the possibility of wide variation in the use of 'TIC' and other 'indirect' methods of detection. Mawby's study in Sheffield found that 40 per cent of offences were cleared in these ways, a figure in excess of that in our research (Mawby, 1979). John Lambert, noting the widespread use of 'TIC' in his study of property crime, made the following remark:

> It is surely curious that the only measure of police efficiency, and one that is widely publicised, is very dependent upon the whim of offenders declaring their interest in previous exploits ... This dependence on getting offenders to confess to maintain a success rate has, I believe, important consequences for police administration and organisation. (Lambert, 1970, p. 43)

Skolnick has examined some of these possible consequences and suggested that admission to past offences can become a valued commodity for exchange. In return the detective may offer reduction of charges, counts and thus indirectly of sentences, and virtual freedom from future arrest for past offences. He suggests that defendants may admit to crimes they have not committed since liability does not increase by doing so, and advantages may well result. He adds that it is possible that some defendants who confess to large numbers of crimes will be shown more leniency in prosecution than those confessing to fewer crimes. Skolnick argues that such consequences should not be seen as symptoms of personal deficiency on the part of detectives or 'efficiency experts' but: 'the problem stems from the well motivated attempts of such experts to develop measurable standards of efficiency. Unfortunately, meeting these standards tends to become an end in itself ...' (Skolnick, 1966, p. 181)

The problem of interpreting changes in a department's clear-up rate becomes even more acute when it is remembered that police practices can also have considerable impact on the figure of reported crime, which can of course have its own effect on the clear-up rate. But the existence of a large but unpredictable number of what have been called 'indirect' detections in the clear-up rate poses serious problems for the use of that figure as a measure of police performance:

> In the London area for example, the number of crimes taken into consideration by the courts is minimal, but this does not mean that in *direct* detective work the Metropolitan and City of London police forces are less effective than other police forces ... (McClintock and Avison, 1968, p. 115)

For this reason, these authors suggest that a 'relative detection rate' should be calculated, which would exclude offences cleared-up by 'indirect methods' from the total of crimes known and those cleared-up. However, even if such rates could be calculated on a regular basis, and other procedural sources of variation could somehow be eliminated, the outlook for the revised rate as an indicator of efficiency still seems in serious doubt:

> When such influences on detection rates are less pronounced

some attempt could perhaps be made to assess influence of socio-economic changes in an area, the growth of criminogenic population groups or conditions, or an increase in kinds of crime that by their nature are more difficult to detect. Only at that point might it be possible to use crime detection rates as reliable indicators of actual or relative efficiency of police forces. (McClintock and Avison, 1968, p. 104—5).

The point is, of course, that not only is it extremely difficult to eliminate procedural sources of variation within what is essentially a 'low visibility' occupation, but that many other varied, and unknown sources of variation are beyond the control of the police, and in the present state of knowledge, beyond the capacity of the statistician to take fully into account.

Table 5.4 summarises the contribution which the various processes discussed so far made to the clear-up rate in our sample of *detected* cases. Firstly we can see that the police were able to observe the offence, or arrive at the scene while the offence was still in progress in 11 per cent of cases. In a further 2 per cent of cases the offender was still present at the scene, although the offence had been committed. More striking are the 9 per cent of cases where the offender was detained by a special agent, usually a store detective, and a further 4 per cent of cases where the offender was detained at the scene the crime by other members of the public. Thus in 26 per cent of detected cases the police were presented with ready-made clear-ups at the scene of the crime, and thus 'real' detective work was unnecessary.

Secondly there are the 'indirect' methods of detection already discussed. All but 12 of those listed as 'admitted under police questioning' were cleared by the 'TIC' mechanism, while a further 1 per cent were cleared by admissions from persons serving custodial sentences. In our experience many of these were cases that the police had found extremely difficult to solve by other methods. They were cleared on paper by a permissible technicality combined with the predicament of certain apprehended persons, and could not usually be regarded as 'detection' in the same sense as other methods.

Thirdly, a striking feature of the table is the figure of 24 per cent for cases in which clear-ups were achieved by means of information from complainants, victims or witnesses. Such a figure underlines the fact that clear-up rates are as much indicators of the behaviour of members of the public as they are of the police, especially since in many cases suspects were *named*.

Finally, if we ignore those cases where information was not available or where the offender gave himself up, the remainder of the sources of detection correspond much more closely to the public

Table 5.4
Prime source of detection

	Cases	
	No.	%
Police observe/discover	115	11
Set up or plant	16	2
Police vigilance	32	3
Offender present when police arrive	24	2
Enquiries	18	2
Information received	56	5
Admitted under questioning (includes 'TIC')	270	26
Admitted while serving custodial sentence	12	1
Information from complainant/victim/witness	242	24
Detained by complainant/victim/witness	44	4
Detained by special agent	97	9
Offender gives himself up	18	2
Not known	78	8
Total	1,022	100

stereotype of 'real detective work'. Yet the contributions of these seems surprisingly small when compared to the other methods we have considered. Our category of 'information received' includes information from contacts, informants, or formal and informal police intelligence systems, and accounts for 5 per cent of detections. Special police enquiries—of which so much are made in the mass media—including fingerprinting, forensic tests, house to house enquiries, apparently made very little contribution by themselves to the clearing-up of the bulk of crime (2 per cent). In fact it was more noticeable how often such techniques were used without success. While the 'set-up' or 'plant' is fairly self explanatory and contributed 2 per cent of clear-ups, police vigilance (3 per cent) is less so. These were cases where offences which had already been reported were cleared because of the powers of observation and quick wittedness of police officers, e.g. stolen goods spotted in a passing vehicle. Such clear-ups were highly valued within the force as 'good police work', and surely deserve greater emphasis in any attempt to evaluate police skills.

These findings indicate that most clear-ups are provided by a suspect being available at the scene of the crime, for a variety of reasons, or by routine questioning of victims and members of the public (see also Greenwood, et al., 1977, p. 225). If crimes are not 'solved' at an early stage, they are likely to remain undetected, unless almost fortuitously cleared at a later stage by an 'indirect' method such as 'TIC'. A proportion of crimes are cleared by direct detective work in which the police take a proactive stance, but this must be placed in focus by remembering the investigative activities which do not lead to clear-ups, and the great part of a detective's time which is spent on activities not related to clear-ups as such, Greenwood, (1977, p.230), has suggested that investigators spend about 93 per cent of their time on activities that do not lead directly to the clearance of reported crime. This suggests that clear-up rates do not reflect adequately what the police actually do, and must therefore be a highly partial measure of police performance. Furthermore, the emphasis on the clear-up rate may lead to a conception of other aspects of the job as not 'real' police work, but 'merely' public relations, paperwork, 'red-tape', 'social work' and so on, which may therefore be resented and/or neglected. This point of course brings us right back to our view that any single measure of police effectiveness can prejudge the issue, both for the police and public, of what the *aims* of police work are or should be. And where a single goal is extolled above all others, this may be at the expense of close scrutiny of the means by which that goal is sought.

Conclusion

In Britain we have been recently reminded of the political humbug that still surrounds the issue of police effectiveness in the struggle to maintain 'law-'n'-order' by the campaign leading up to the general election of May 1979. It is in situations of this kind that advantage may be taken of the widespread ignorance of basic truths about the growth of crime and the limitations (in this context) of police work. Thus it is more than ever necessary to attempt to dispel such ignorance and expose the extent of political and professional double-talk. There should be no need for the police role in the war against crime to become a political football, whether to gain votes or to improve pay and conditions. Such distortions ultimately undermine an appreciation of the real nature of police work and achievements.

Official crime rates, despite all their limitations, are likely to remain the basic source for public perceptions of the 'crime problem' and police effectiveness for many years to come. For this reason alone they must be subject to constant scrutiny. In particular, their internal significance within the context of day-to-day police decision-making must not be ignored; so often they can most appropriately be viewed as the *product* of a decision that has already been taken or the *reflection* of a judgement that has already been arrived at, whether in terms of arresting a suspect, despatching a patrol car, sorting out a 'domestic', or whatever; alternatively, for the ordinary police officer they can constitute an 'account' to his superiors of how his time has been spent. These 'latent' functions of the production of crime rates should be more openly acknowledged.

However, from the perspective of the researcher, the evidence presented in this paper indicates the need for specially collected research data in order to evaluate aspects of police performance in any precise manner. Even here there is a basic need to be able to assume that other conditions that might affect the data are constant so that the 'experimental' factor is the only one that varies. The possible range of such conditions means that this is a far more difficult task than is commonly realised. For example we have seen how new police methods might result in increased public reporting of crime, thereby masking any primary effects in reducing criminal behaviour itself.

Finally, the focus of the public debate about crime and the police should be switched from limited and relatively imprecise measures of alleged 'effectiveness', to an examination of the broader issue of the *objectives of policing* and *public expectations*. The police are more likely to raise themselves in the public estimation by improving their visibility, accessibility and the quality of their 'after-sales' service when complaints have been received or crimes reported. Working *with the public* in this way, as a prime objective in its own right, might pave the way for a new conception of *shared responsibility* for law and order, not measured by highly dubious crime statistics but in terms of a realistic assessment of the nature of the crime, order and dispute settlement in society:

> ... the critical need is to improve the quality and quantity of police-citizen interaction. This must be a central task, not for the purpose of improving the police image but rather to encourage the normal social control exercised by a healthy community. The police must be seen as only an aid to the community, as the community itself deals with social problems. The police certainly are essential, but *policing* is too important to be left to the police alone. (Kelling, 1978, p. 184)

Note

This chapter is based on research financed by the Social Science Research Council.

References

Belson, W. A., (1975), *Juvenile Theft: the Causal Factors,* Harper and Row, London.

Biderman, A. D., (1967), *Report on a Pilot Study in the District of Columbia on Victimisation and Attitudes toward Law Enforcement,* in President's Commission on Law Enforcement and Administration of Justice, *Field Surveys I,* US Government Printing Office, Washington, DC.

Black, D. J., (1970), 'Production of crime rates', *American Sociological Review,* 35, pp. 733—48.

Black, D. J., (1971), 'The social organisation of arrest', *Stanford Law Review,* 23, pp. 1087—1111.

Bordua, D. J., and Tifft, L. L., (1971), 'Citizen interviews, organisational feedback and police-community relations decisions', *Law and Society Review,* 6, pp. 155—82.

Bottomley, A. K., and Coleman, C. A., (1976), 'Criminal statistics: the police role in the discovery and detection of crime', *International Journal of Criminology and Penology,* 4, pp. 33—58.

Bottomley, A. K., and Coleman, C. A., (in press), *Understanding Crime Rates,* Saxon House, Farnborough.

Center, L. J., and Smith, T. G., (1973), 'Crime statistics—can they be trusted?', *American Criminal Law Review,* 11, pp. 1045—86.

Chartered Institute of Public Finance and Accountancy, (1978), *Police Statistics: Estimates: 1978/79,* CIPFA Statistical Information Service, London.

Chatterton, M., (1976), 'Police in social control', in King, J. F. S., (ed.), *Control without Custody?,* Institute of Criminology, Cambridge.

Clarke, R. V. G., and Heal, K. H., (1979), 'Police effectiveness in dealing with crime: some current British research', *The Police Journal,* 52, pp. 24—41.

Coleman, C. A., and Bottomley, A. K., (1976), 'Police conceptions of crime and "no crime" ' *Criminal Law Review,* pp. 344—60.

Conklin, J. E., (1975), *The Impact of Crime,* Collier - Macmillan, London.

Conklin, J. E., and Bittner, E., (1973), 'Burglary in a suburb', *Criminology,* 11, pp. 206—32.

Elliott, J. F., (1978), 'Crime control teams: an alternative to the conventional operational procedure of investigating crimes', *Journal of Criminal Justice,* 6, pp. 11—23.

Ferracuti, F., Hernandez, R., and Wolfgang, M., (1962), 'A study of police errors in crime classification', *Journal of Criminal Law*

Criminology and Police Science, 53, pp. 113—19.

Furstenberg, F. F., and Wellford, C. F., (1973), 'Calling the police: the evaluation of police service', *Law and Society Review,* 7, pp. 393—406.

Greenwood, P. W., Chaiken, J. M., Petersilia, J., (1977), *The Criminal Investigation Process,* D. C. Heath, Lexington, Mass.

Home Office, (1971), *Instructions for the Preparation of Statistics Relating to Crime,* Home Office, London.

Kelling, G. L., (1978), 'Police field services and crime: the presumed effects of a capacity, *Crime and Delinquency,* 24, pp. 173—83.

Kelling, G. L., Pate, T., Dieckman, D., and Brown, C. E., (1974), *The Kansas City Preventive Patrol Experiment,* Police Foundation, Washington, DC.

Lambert, J. R., (1970), *Crime, Police and Race Relations,* Oxford University Press, London.

Littrell, W. B., (1973), 'Vagueness, social structure, and social research in law', *Social Problems,* 21, pp. 38—48.

McCabe, S., and Sutcliffe, F., (1978), *Defining Crime: A Study of Police Decisions,* Blackwell, Oxford.

McClintock, F. H., and Gibson, E., (1961), *Robbery in London,* Macmillan, London.

McClintock, F. H., (1963), *Crimes of Violence,* Macmillan, London.

McClintock, F. H., and Avison, N. H., (1968), *Crime in England and Wales,* Heinemann, London.

Mawby, R. I., (1979), *Policing the City,* Saxon House, Farnborough.

Morrisey, W. R., (1972), 'Nixon anti-crime plan undermines crime stats', *Justice Magazine,* June/July issue, pp. 8—11.

Pepinsky, H. E., (1976), 'Police patrolmen's offence-reporting behaviour', *Journal of Research in Crime and Delinquency,* 13, pp. 33—47.

Schnelle, J. F., Kirchner, R. E., McNees, M. P., and Lawler, J. M., (1975), 'Social evaluation research: the evaluation of two police patrolling strategies', *Journal of Applied Behavior Analysis,* 8, pp. 353—65.

Seidman, D., and Couzens, M., (1974), 'Getting the crime rate down: political pressure and crime reporting', *Law and Society Review,* 8, pp. 457—93.

Sellin, T., and Wolfgang, M. E., (1964), *The Measurement of Delinquency,* Wiley, New York.

Skogan, W. G., (1975), 'Public policy and public evaluations of criminal justice system performance', in Gardiner, J. S., and Mulkey, M. A., (eds.), *Crime and Criminal Justice: Issues in Public Policy Analysis,* D. C. Heath, Lexington, Mass.

Skolnick, J. H., (1966), *Justice Without Trial: Law Enforcement in*

Democratic Society, Wiley, New York.

Sparks, R. F., Genn, H., and Dodd, D., (1977), *Surveying Victims*, Wiley, London.

Tanner, R. E. S., (1970), *Three Studies in East African Criminology*, Scandinavian Institute of African Studies, Uppsala.

West, D. J., and Farrington, D. P., (1973), *Who Becomes Delinquent?*, Heinemann, London.

Wilson, J. Q., (1975), *Thinking About Crime*, Basic Books, New York.

Zander, M., (1979), 'The investigation of crime: a study of cases tried at the Old Bailey', *Criminal Law Review*, pp. 203—19.

6 Organisation and environment: influences on police work

Peter K. Manning

The police and the environment

All occupations and organisations that serve the public encounter and must resolve in some fashion the tension that results from two often quite distinct sources of demand: the external sources arising from the expressed demands of clients, patients, citizens or patrons, and the internally generated 'survival interests' of the organisation. All organisations are similarly shaped (see, for example, Gouldner, 1959; Selznick, 1966; Hughes, 1971).

In the study of the police, there are two rather different interpretations of the relationship between the police and the environment. One interpretation emphasises the capacity of the police, through the paramilitary structure of command and control, to shape, pattern and respond to citizen demand in a fashion that mediates or at least maintains the autonomy of the organisation. Another interpretation sees far greater citizen control over the police, and in fact argues that the essential determining forces are patterns of citizen demand. This paper reviews these arguments, presents some data on police responses to citizen demand, and assesses these two rather polar positions.

It has been argued that the police have been shaped historically by the administrative and ultimately political aim of maintaining control over officers such that the demands of the public for service would be received, responded to neutrally and expeditiously, and duty assigned would be performed without regard to personal considerations. In the classic Weberian conception of bureaucracy, the expectation is that an obligation to obedience would predominate over other considerations in the execution of police duties (Weber, 1947, pp. 330 ff.).   Reith (1943) claims that one of the purposes of the early innovators in the organisation of the police (Peel, the Fieldings, Rowan and Mayne) was to create an organisational form which would provide service while preserving the political autonomy and the integrity of the police organisation. Thus, in effect, it is argued that the police evolved to the present organisational form through control of the environment (demand). This conception is indeed fundamental to police histories, and the overall premise guiding the analysis of the development of the police is one of documenting increasing rationality, professionalism, and accomplishment (e.g., Reith, 1943; Bordua, 1968; Miller, 1977).

The mechanism through which this neutral control over the demand issuing from the environment is said to be accomplished is the 'quasi-military' or 'paramilitary' model. The features of the paramilitary model of policing, with its rigid rank structure, strict lines of command and control, a sharply drawn division of labour symbolic paraphernalia serving to mark levels of authority and responsibility, impersonality and a rational and integrating communication system linking the levels of the organisation and the organisation and the environment, are frequently characterised in social science literature (e.g., Niederhoffer, 1967; McNamara, 1967; Wilson and McLaren, 1972, Cain, 1973). The assumption is made that in addition to political neutrality the probability of which is increased by such control systems, these internal attributes also facilitate the capacity of the police to respond differentially to a number of diverse kinds of events. Not only are these events unpredictable in their appearance, their duration, scope and intensity, they are in some sense statistically independent. The paramilitary model aims to interpose a controlling administrative structure between aggregated citizen demand and the police response.

The well nurtured hope that the police in both the United States and in England might become more effective in their roles as crime-fighters and thief-takers is based on the assumption that the structure of policing is such that major increments in their performance can be achieved through administrative command and control. Police claims to be crime-fighters are validated by segments of the public who believe that the police should be crime-fighters. The emphasis on crime-fighting work, from the police point of view, is readily understandable. Crime work is less controversial than other police functions, solidifies middle class support of the police, amplifies many of the aspirations of officers, is glamorous and attractive, and reifies the police into a unit with a single dominant function. Many researchers, in turn, have equated effectiveness of the police with their crime related functions, and in a strange semantic twist, claim that effectiveness in the crime domain is equivalent to organisational effectiveness (Chaiken, 1978). In effect, many police researchers have accepted the validity and veridicality of the paramilitary model and asked how more effective crime control might be achieved. (See the useful review of productivity studies done by O'Connor and Gilman, 1978.)

An argument placing more emphasis on citizen demand in shaping policing is based on the assumption that the police are tightly coupled to the environment. This model posits *tight coupling* between the organisation and the environment such that a given level of 'inputs' of citizen co-operation, information, equipment, personnel, and money will produce a given level of 'outputs' such as arrests. An example of this conceptualisation is found in an essay by Reiss and Bordua (1967). They argue that the municipal police operate as an organisational system, and they emphasise the significance of '... its relations with the organised environment and its boundary transactions and ... internal differentiation [of the police system] and problems of integration, co-ordination and control' (1967, p. 25). They expand this perspective further by noting that the organisation transacts and deploys its resources in response to the demands of the environment, and this adaptation and adjustment permits even closer transactional relationships between the (crime) environment and the police organisation. They urge the consideration of a general proposition about policing which well captures the assumption of tight coupling:

> ... quite clearly both the volume of the crime known to the police and the proportion cleared by arrest is some function of how much resources it takes to gain knowledge of a particular crime and clear it by arrest. No department can exceed its resource capacity. Since beyond a certain point the amount of resources necessary to clear a crime exceeds the willingness of society to allocate additional resources, it is not surprising that three out of every four crimes known to the police will remain unsolved. One caveat, of course, must be entered to such a statement. There undoubtedly are, in the nature of the case, a large number of crimes that will remain unsolved regardless of the resources allocated to their solution, since information required to solve them can never become available in the police system. No police department can know more crime than its resources make possible for it to know in that given period of time nor solve more than its resources make possible. From a social organisational point of view, the crime in any social system is a function of the organisational capabilities to know it. (Reiss and Bordua, 1967, p. 47)

The demand conditions in the environment are thus converted and transformed rationally to achieve organisational goals such as reduced crime, increased citizen satisfaction, increased clearance rate for investigated crimes, increased arrests, etc.

Neither of these positions clarifies the question of the *degree* of shaping that the environment or demand has upon police practice and structure. Both have noted, sometimes in great detail, that the discretion of lower participants, the lack of policy, the uncertain appearance of the situations encountered, the diversity of the tasks involved, and the ambiguity of the situations and the judgements required, tend to contradict the centrally controlled, articulated, co-ordinated multiple-level system depicted in the paramilitary imagery. The question to be addressed is to what extent is citizen *demand* determinant of policing, and to what extent does the police organisation shape, create, and maintain dominant control over demand? This question antedates the issue of whether the police can control crime, function as a social service agency, or the like.

It is hoped that this paper will bear on basic management questions in the police field. Police function has been examined in recent research in the Unites States and in England focusing on the demand for service. This research concerns in part the information processing structures of the police. Such data should provide a means by which to assess or characterise some determinants of the level of police service. If the ways in which the demand of citizens is shaped can be identified, then the implications for management should follow logically. If they are responsive primarily to the environment, then rational management plans can have only marginal effect, given the present structure of policing. If, on the other hand, the police systematically disattach themselves from the environment, and strive to maintain power and autonomy, then other management approaches are necessary.

Aspects of environment-organisation interchange

In order to evaluate the argument that the police are dependent on the citizens and that citizen demand shapes police practice, it would be useful to have full data on the nature of the demand that police receive, including citizen calls, planned demand that the police respond to as a result of anticipated needs in the community such as scheduled events, e.g., parades, demonstrations, football matches, etc., and the demand that is created in a sense by police definition of problems in the community that need their attention. Under this category are such things as a series of burglaries or robberies in an area, citizen concern about rapes or drug use which police attempt to control by special task forces, concentration of personnel or the like.

However, these data are not presently available for social science researchers. We have studies such as Reiss' (1971, p. 11), which show that for a sample of high crime precincts in the United States some 87 per cent of all police mobilisations are the result of citizens' calls. These dispatched calls, however, make up only 14 per cent of patrol time (85 per cent is devoted to 'routine patrol', 1 per cent to self-initiated activities). A series of studies of calls for assistance and of dispatch have been made and will be discussed in detail below. In addition, there are some data that have been gathered recently by the author in a small pilot study of a large Midwestern police department. These data include observations of dispatch practices, interviews with officers, operators and administrative personnel, and observation of officers in the field. Some of these data will be used to provide examples of dispatching in large urban areas in the United States. (Some similarities may be found with the 999 system in London, although this is only speculation on my part at this point.) They illuminate the effects of the communications system on demand.

In any information system there are critical decision points at which the level of information changes radically in one direction or the other. In a police communication system, there are a number of such key points as shown in Table 6.1. From the major studies of dispatch and calls made to the police (Cumming, et al., 1965; Wilson, 1968; Martin, 1969; Bercal, 1970; Reiss, 1971; Webster, 1973; Lilly, 1978; Cordner, 1979), it is known that many calls are lost at each stage in the process. If the system uses a general service number such as has been established in the States (911), many calls are referred to other systems (fire, emergency medical service, social welfare, etc.), and many calls are irrelevant to police action (harrassing calls, wrong numbers such as callers who intended to call 411 or 611 information or telephone service). There are no data at present about what proportion of all calls are handled by the police, nor what proportion of all calls are defined as relevant by the operator or the dispatcher. From dispatch studies, it is known that somewhere between 30 and 70 per cent of all calls are handled by the dispatcher without sending a vehicle.

Table 6.1

A taxonomy of calls for service

Calls made	Calls sent to dispatcher
Calls lost in queue	Calls received by dispatcher(s)
Calls lost at 911 level	Calls recoded (type)
Calls referred (previous call, repeat)	Calls dispatched (type)
Calls transferred (EMS, fire)	Calls received by units (type)
Calls accepted by operators	Calls completed (type)
Calls coded for action (type)	Calls in activity logs
Internal calls	

The systems used by different studies and different police departments to classify calls are non-comparable, as Cordner (1979, p. 7) notes:

102

A major problem in comparing the findings of the various patrol workload studies is the wide variety and activity categories used. Of the thirteen studies reviewed, eleven group patrol activity data into seven or fewer categories (the categories used in the other two studies were very narrow in scope, and not considered in this discussion). Between these eleven studies, 38 clearly distinct categories were used. Although the categories are not always well defined in the studies, from the descriptions and examples provided it can be concluded that the diverse classification schemes used are very different and very difficult to compare.

Comparison between citizens' definitions of the nature of their calls, and the police recoding of those calls has been revealing undertaken by Reiss (1971), on the basis of a sample of calls to the Chicago, Illinois Police Department for April 1966. Reiss found that although the citizens defined some 58 per cent of their calls as crime-related, the police dispatched on all these calls—and these crime-related calls were a majority of the calls dispatched—but the police themselves defined only 17 per cent of their dispatches as crime-related. Fully 83 per cent of patrol calls were defined as 'non-criminal', with 'miscellaneous' (41 per cent) and 'disturbances' (25 per cent) as large subcategories.

Underlying the analysis of any message are the bases of *trust* that are involved in receiving, evaluating and processing a call. For example, in the Midwestern Police Department, there is a 'phony runs' book which contains addresses to which units have been dispatched maliciously (e.g., teenagers who want to harass a neighbour), to create problems (e.g., a dope pad), or by persons who are 'crazy' or 'lonely' or 'want attention'. These addresses are written on a blackboard so that operators can distrust them immediately and terminate the request from the caller. Since officially all calls are answered, this procedure creates a number of logical contradictions within the system. Distrust of citizen calls is obviously one reason why calls are never dispatched. This was profoundly true in drug enforcement where the primary concern of the officer was not the content of the call, but the *credibility* of the caller. Reiss (1971, p. 13) suggests this is also true of central dispatch in Chicago, and our observations sustain the fact that this freedom to distrust the content of the message increases as one moves to 'the street'. Once inside the system, enormous latitude is permitted to police participants to redefine with impunity the nature of the claims upon assistance from citizens. Let us examine the sources and kinds of discretion available.

In the Midwestern Department the greatest degree of discretion is found among the officers on the street, while the least is found among the 911 operators. Dispatchers, sworn officers doing 'non-police work', stand midway between the two. This is so for several reasons, in addition to the fact that the 911 operators are civilian and female (about 95 per cent), dispatchers are sworn officers and male (about 85 per cent) and officers are sworn and male (about 88 per cent).

One source of discretion is the degree to which technology controls the *flow* of the work at each of the three levels: calls are routed to the operators *in order* as operators become free; they have no choice, nor any way to anticipate the arrival, nature of, or interval between calls. After receiving the caller's information, they remain out of service (unavailable for calls) until they transmit the message to a dispatcher. They must send one message to the dispatcher before they receive another. (They are literally and technologically 'out of service' until they punch back in after the call has been terminated or sent.) They must type in a valid address or location (cross streets) before the computer with a screen that is their data-processing terminal will permit them to enter further information. After a message is sent, the computer shows whether it has been received or confirmed by the dispatcher's computer. Their breaks are strictly controlled, 900 seconds in each hour (monitored by a computer). They cannot alter the priorities of events but can set priority sensitivities by the code they select to which to assign a call. When they receive multiple reports on an event (wire down in an alley, broken water main, fire), they must receive all of them and compose a message reporting that a unit is *en route*. Their greatest source of discretion lies in their freedom in assigning codes to events; they must convert the message into one of the available 245 codes. Sensing and sorting based on their image of the event, their readings of tone of voice, and facts given are all useful. However, they tend to treat the *order of calls* as the primary demand condition, and the level of work is the most important determinant of discretion. This contrasts, it appears, to the situation of the dispatchers and the officers in cars.

Dispatchers assigned to police zones in the city, once they have a call in hand do not have to respect the priorities given an event by the 911 operators; they do not have to accept the next card sent by the operators until they are ready. It can remain with several others or be placed in a stack in front of the dispatcher. They receive only calls to their zone, although like the 911 people, they cannot anticipate when the next call will come, what its nature will be, or what the intervals will be between subsequent calls, e.g., whether they might be overloaded in the next few minutes. They can work with any of several calls in front of them and try to reach any of several cars (in or out of service). They can talk back and forth with the receiver of the message (the 911 people are told not to call dispatchers, and rarely do, although dispatchers call 911 people). They can change assignments made to one car to another, or terminate a request. They are not governed by the computer. The radio is a controlling channel. It provides two-way peer communication because it can both go out and come into the dispatchers from the cars. Calls are also received by dispatchers on the police phone (internal) and from outside lines as well (some calls are screened). Unlike the 911 people, who can only accept calls, terminate calls that are meant for 411 (information) or 611 (telephone repair), children playing on the phone or other nuisance calls, or are terminated by callers, or refer, dispatchers can juggle more than one call at a time, shift priorities, and alter event codes (they can write a new code directly on the card). These actions enable them to maintain autonomy from demands of the machines and the calls routed to them from 911 operators. The level of work is generally low, but varies by time of day, day of the week, and month. Their breaks are set but not monitored by a computer (they write their own in and out times on a log book beside the console). In general, they work in terms of a metaphor or paradigmatic conception of the meaning of the calls rather than the order in which they are received (metonymy). They define them as either priority, (usually involving danger and crime-relatedness) and 'other' calls or 'real' versus 'non-police' work (see below).

Officers have the greatest degree of discretion, as has been frequently noted. It should be mentioned that seniority is the basis for assigning officers to cars (that is, it is the basis of assignment to areas since cars are based in areas within each precinct). Although officers within the precincts know who is in each car, the dispatchers do not. Thus observations made by Rubinstein (1973) and Chatterton (1973) concerning the significance of personal knowledge and relationships between officers and dispatchers is not relevant in this city. There are too many officers, the turnover rate in the dispatchers in the centre is too high, and officers do not dispatch in the same zones that they might have worked in as officers. They do not, therefore, necessarily know the city in detail in the area for which they are controller.

They have choice in accepting calls offered to them (when a general call is issued) and even when called for, because the dispatcher cannot know when they are busy or out of radio contact.

They can respond to calls to which they were not assigned, even those out of their sector or precinct. They can drop assignments for a 'hot call' with impunity. Since they do not have to call in when they arrive on the scene, but only have to report in when they are 'clear' there is no independent way to establish where a car is, or what assignment it might be on (except by what is shown on the cards in the dispatchers' slots). They can juggle more than one call at a time, alter priorities or assignments, such as taking one call when on the way to another, taking a call while transporting a prisoner or leaving one scene after accepting a call to another (especially on a chase, or officer in trouble, or crime-in-progress call). They do not have to accept the code assigned to the event by the 911 operator or dispatcher, because they can enter in their activity logs what appears to be reasonable. The computer print-out for the calls dispatched and received at 911 does not include the disposition of the call. It shows only that a car accepted the call (and at what time), and at what time the car called in as being clear. Their level of work is uneven, by shift, area, and day of the week, and time of the day. They can either 'make work' by checking the 'hot' sheet, looking for stolen cars, talking with informants, etc., or they can avoid it by being out of radio contact or 'easing' (Cain, 1973). Their breaks are non-routine in fact, even where regulations govern their length. They only have to say 'show me busy' and get a confirmation from the dispatcher to be out of service (research shows about 20 per cent of time is devoted to non-police activities). Finally, they view their work in terms similar to the dispatchers, as metaphoric: in general terms as 'shit work' or 'non-crime' work versus 'real police work' of various kinds. They are not tied to the next call, even when very busy, as the above shows.

Most importantly, discretion in the delivery system aside, it must be appreciated that virtually all these calls are ambiguous when received by the operators. Some suggestions of this ambiguity and the mode of analysis which might be attempted can be indicated, if we conceived of these events in behavioural terms. This analysis, it would appear, suggests that not only is demand shaped by the decisions made within the delivery system by officers most particularly, but that the incoming calls are themselves so diverse as to content and meaning that they can be almost infinitely redefined by context and order (this argument is detailed in the final section of the paper). By looking at these calls as behavioural events one can see that the content of the demand is perhaps as significant as the load itself.

One of the difficulties in analysing or comparing data from police departments on calls served, crimes solved and investigated, and information processed is that the behavioural events brought to the attention of the police are never simply 'raw stimuli', but are always sensed and sorted out (typified as kinds of calls), put into formal codes (used by communications centres for dispatching purposes and internal record keeping), and processed from one stage in the communication system to another. Two main effects will be discussed here. The first is the translation and back-translation of various behavioural events reported to the police into codable and actionable police-understood codes and meanings. The other is the effect of order on meaning and priority of events. An example will perhaps be useful to illustrate this process:

A bartender (publican) calls the police department on Friday night and complains of a fight between several men with weapons in his establishment, and requests police assistance at a given place, address, and time. There are at least ten received separate informational bits that can be used to classify that call at the 911 subsystem level. Let us display them as follows: (a) fight; (b) bar disturbance; (c) time of call; (d) the named place—the Dew Drop Inn; (e) address—626 Kazimeir Street; (f) neighbourhood— area; (g) bartender (role); (h) bartender's name, age and sex; (i) size of the disturbance; (j) presence/absence of weapons. There are, in addition, a number of contextual understandings that can be 'read off' from (or 'read into') the information in the call such as: (1) the previous history of fights in that bar; (2) the neighbourhood and its potential for sparking further disturbances; (3) the time of day as related to the tours of duty of officers and whether they are or will be available to handle the disturbance; (4) the past history of the bartender's calling for help (whether he/she is known to the operator, dispatchers or officers); (5) the vulnerability of the bartender, especially as understood in terms of age (older or very young people are more vulnerable), sex (women are more vulnerable), any relevant personal characteristics e.g., a crippled person calling; (6) the larger the disturbance, the more dangerous; (7) whether the call is a day time, early evening or night time call is related to the type of clientele, their potential for fighting, and the number of people in the bar; (8) day of the week—Friday and Saturday nights are typically more volatile, in part because people have been paid and may drink as a result.

Only a few preliminary comments can be made concerning the ambiguities of processing:

1 If the sum of the information bits rendered to the operator are a-j, that in this example, any one of four bits of information can be used to classify the event (refer to the Midwestern codes listed in the Appendix).

Bit		Code	Name	Subcode
a	=	34	(assault)	1-3401, 2-3402
b	=	82	(disturbance)	3-8210, 3-8230, 3-8270
c	=	84	(persons)	3-8400, 3-8410
j	=	34	(assault-weapon codes)	1-3431, 1-3461

2 Formal priorities (e.g., 1-3401; 2-3402, and 3-8410) are printed out preceding the event codes.
3 The remarks typed below the message sent by 911 operators to dispatchers indicate the priority-related meanings listed above in 1-8. These remarks could, of course, be used at any point along the line to change the meaning, priority and event classification of any given event, no matter what the original code or demand of the caller.
4 These meanings change over time and from subsystem to subsystem since the codes and priorities can change and the negative feedback capacity is limited.
5 The particular bit of information (a-j) that is salient, if message content is the orientation of the receiver, can change the nature of the event. There are no rules for choosing between the items focused on, or within the categories (e.g., 3401 v. 3402), except what the operator makes of the message given by the caller.
6 The stored facts (kept in the computer memory and easily retrieved and shown on the 911 operator's screen) which the operator and no one else in the system knows, i.e., the last five calls nearest the address or location given in the previous 24 hours, may also function as priority-meaning data. For example, if the call is the third one in the last few minutes from that address, it is referred, not forwarded to the dispatcher. Thus, each message has not only a fact and context aspect, but a temporal or sequential aspect which patterns its significance and meaning.

There is an effect, as noted above, of the actual *sequencing* of the calls received by persons at each level in the system. The importance of sequencing is differential, however, depending on the subsystem in which one is located. Generally, the 911 operators are oriented to the *metonymic* aspects of the communication sequence (the order in which the calls are received). They must take one call before they take another, are given the calls mechanically, one after another, as soon as they are back in service, and they must code the event in one and only one code. Dispatchers are oriented to both the order and the clustered meanings of calls (the *metaphoric* aspects of the communication). The scout car operators are oriented almost entirely to the metaphoric aspects of the messages (the similarity in meaning of the calls, given the context in which they are received). This process can be illustrated by the following hypothetical sequence of eleven calls received by a 911 operator:

1   1-3511, Breaking and entering, in progress.
2   1-3941, Family trouble, fight.
3   3-8270, Disturbance/trouble.
4   4-8469, Missing report.
5   1-3101, Robbery in progress.
6   Wrong number.
7   Nuisance call—obscene harassment.
8   Called before—refer.
9   3-3532, Breaking and entering auto—just happened.
10 3-3740, Investigate auto.
11 1-9000, Officer in trouble.

For the operator, all but numbers 6, 7 and 8 *must* be sent, and the priority is automatically set, given selection of a code. The content of the calls has no bearing on the operator's workload, priorities, or the significance of the next call. Meaning is almost entirely given by the temporal sequence of calls or metonymy.

The same eleven calls can be classified for administrative purposes to generate crime or service-given statistics, or calls listed as received under at least three metaphoric orderings:

1 *Person v. property related incidents*
Person incidents: numbers 2, 3, 4, 5 and 11
Property related incidents: numbers 1, 9 and 10

2 *'Crime' v. 'non-crime' incidents*
Crime: numbers 1, 5 and 9
Non-crime: numbers 6, 7, 8 (2, 3, 4, 10 and 11)
Possible crime: numbers 2, 3, 4, 10 and 11

3 *Potential for arrest—Action (need for speed)*
Rush: numbers 1, 3, 5 and 11
Non-rush: numbers 2, 4, and 10 (6, 7 and 8—not known to
    officers and dispatchers).

It should be emphasised that although calls in this system are given a priority, these priorities are altered at each stage in the communications system. Of the calls dispatched in the several studies of dispatch, it is clear that a high percentage of these are

109

ambiguous, even given the category to which they are assigned by dispatchers or by social researchers. Obviously, then, aspects of the situation other than the dispatch message itself shape the response that is made to the call. Note that the metonymic ordering of the dispatchers is converted by the officers into a metaphoric ordering because they have discretion to alter the order of the calls to which they attend. Reiss found that the police viewed 73 per cent of all calls as 'routine', and proceeded at normal speed without lights or siren. The impact of priorities on officer behaviour is not well researched, but evidence from Larson, et al. (1978) and Bieck (1977), shows that priorities set by dispatchers did not alter the response time of the vehicles, even when automatic vehicle locators which emit signals from a transmitter in the car were used to monitor performance. Anomalous responses mentioned by Bieck, and often observed by others (Manning, 1979b)   result because, as noted below, the *context* of the call is read as giving it more or less immediacy than the official priority or label. Pepinsky's (1976) study found few anomalies between dispatch and officers' actions when an offense was mentioned as central to the incident. This is a small sample of the total range of calls dispatched, and does not reveal understandings other than those conveyed by the verbal message that an offence may be involved. The effects of other meanings are not revealed in Pepinsky's insightful article. The discretion of officers is not shared. For example, the dispatchers have some freedom to alter priorities, but operators do not. Thus, in order to understand the pattern of response, the ordering of calls to attend to, and the quality of the service, one must have information on both the nature of the calls (information bits, priority meanings, and stored facts) *and* the effects of order (metonymy) and meaning (metaphor).

Workload and demand

It should be noted that some studies have found that the workload by units and departments using dispatched calls varies considerably. Data in Table 6.2 show comparisons for two cities in the United States with similar populations. Note that the workload based on the ratio of calls to officers for Pittsburgh over the period 1969 to 1975 is from 1.71 (1975) to 2.44 (1969) times higher than that for the officers in San Antonio, Texas. These data do not inform us of what proportion of the calls for service were never dispatched. It is difficult to determine what the sources of the variation in the service delivered in these two communities are, but it suggests that closer analysis of how the calls are screened within the department might be revealing of policies and patterns of service delivery.

Table 6.2

Workload ratios for two departments†

San Antonio

	(1) Calls for Service*	(2) Uniformed police**	(3) Workload (ratio of (1) to (2))
1969	266,721	849	314.2
1975	371,662	1,175	316.3

Pittsburgh

1969	224,848	1,748	128.6
1975	260,437	1,411	184.6

*From Annual Reports of department.
**From Uniform Crime Report.
†From Henig, et al., (1977).

In a review of dispatch studies Cordner (1979), found that calls that were actually sent to vehicles accounted for somewhere between 40 and 50 per cent of the workload of officers in cars. Small amounts of time are spent on crime-related duties, some 10–20 per cent of the time on non-duty related activities, and finally, a substantial, but variable amount of time is spent on administrative duties (10–50 per cent). A large amount of patrol time is 'driving around time' that is basically uncommitted to any sort of duty.

Finally, if workload studies are closely examined, it is clear that there is a set of unanswered questions and data, especially about the flow-through processing of calls. These have been mistakenly used as indices of the level of demand from the environment. Very often, for example, calls for service are taken from those dispatched by a department, and the original 'raw data' from dispatch tapes are not coded; or the coding procedures are not presented in the published report so that comparisons across studies might be undertaken (cf. Cordner, 1979). 'Calls dispatched' is not a uniform category in the studies for several reasons:

1 Some studies use observations or data from activity logs in cars filled out by officers *after* calls have been accepted.

111

2 Evidence from Reiss suggests that a large number of calls that persons make to the Department were never received, not processed, or not answered by units.

3 Data in the ongoing study of the Midwestern Police Department is kept by the department is such a way that calls dispatched, calls disposed of, and the nature of the disposition cannot be tracked without compiling laboriously three different kinds of records (dispatch, vehicle activity logs, and 911 operators' records that are only kept for 36 hours in the computer).

4 Not all calls dispatched are answered by units.

5 Not all dispositions are recorded or kept in an official record.

6 Routine comparisons of data sets are not done in central communications.

Only as a result of emergency situations are the various sets compared. For example, in the Midwestern department studied, records were not kept by central communications on the disposition of calls. More importantly, no records were kept on whether the call was answered at all except in the sense that the officer accepted the call and radioed in to be cleared. The times of accepting calls and requesting clearance are recorded, as are the conversations between the dispatcher(s) and the officer.

Comments on the effect of the environment on the police

Arguments which assert a high degree of control by citizens over the police probably overstate the case, just as advocates of the paramilitary approach do. The significance of citizen calls for service on the overall pattern of policing is exaggerated. Let us review some support for my claim. Arguments for a degree of control exercised by the citizen are in some sense hypothetical insofar as they note that *if* the citizen does not report the incident, the police might not be able to act. This is true, but on the other hand, this frees the police to act as they choose during the time which they do not devote to the incident. Second, the argument mistakes the *form* of the call for compelling content. Since virtually every call is *transformed* in the course of being transmitted through the system, and redefined at several points, both as it moves vertically and horizontally through the system, the content of calls is in the possession of the police, not the citizen. Third, the calls which are dispatched in any case do not account for more than one-half of the time of officers on patrol: they are free to do as they choose during the remainder of that time. Fourth, while the research of Black and Reiss has shown that citizens exercise control over incidents, one must recall following Black

(1971) that the study of arrests flatters the police, and that their encounters with the citizens in the course of law enforcement is a relatively small portion of their time (10—15 per cent, according to various studies). Fifth, even where the calls involve specific dispatch labels or categories, since there is no feedback that is officially recorded on the incidents in most departments, the prospective control exercised by the organisation and the citizen is minimal. Sixth, as noted in a study of officers in both London and in the United States, the *occupational culture* of the officers provides the dominant context within which calls are seen (Manning, 1979b). Although this proposition can be elaborated and specified, some general points can be made:

(a) Regardless of the present position and activities of an officer, certain events can serve as a warrant for the avoidance, setting-aside, ignoring or otherwise finessing an ongoing assignment (these events are largely crime-related, or officer-in-danger types of calls).

(b) The police expect that they are expected to do something and usually fairly quickly. They read events in this context (Bittner, 1974).

(c) Officers work to do two things: to accomplish work within the premises of the work as they understand them, and to create, if necessary, the proper official paper which will represent events as they are administratively understood (Manning, 1977).

(d) Original alterations of the *pro forma* expectations of patrol are understood in the context of events at hand, and not against a programme, formal set of priorities, or goals established for that time period.

(e) Work must be properly considered team work (Goffman, 1959, p. 104) and the reality of the choices must be communicated to others on the same team (Van Maanen, 1974).

(f) The interests of the officer are primarily to control the scene and to produce outcomes consistent with a definition of what needs doing, deciding whether, what and how to record it. What is written is in part based on 'readings' of the interests of supervising officers.

Seventh, only where paper is written on the disposition of the incident is there a high likelihood of systematic review. Most police departments in the United States do not have citizen review boards and there are virtually no mechanisms for requiring systematic review of police procedures for handling calls short of a civil or criminal suit. Eighth, it has been argued (Reiss and Bordua, 1967; Davis, 1969; Manning, 1979) that the police are overwhelmed or at

113

least *overloaded* with calls which they cannot, given their present level or resources, answer. It has been argued that they cannot answer all the calls directed to them; that they often have calls waiting in queues that are eventually lost, and that they are frequently unable to answer all the calls even those dispatched and accepted by units. (This is the case from time to time in the Midwestern Police Department, where I was told that during summer nights they can run anywhere from one-half to three-quarters of an hour behind the calls accepted for dispatch.) Since, however, the priorities set by operators and dispatchers are non-binding on officers on the ground, officers can establish informal priorities and set an 'invisible agenda'. Demand is essentially demand at the *receiving* end of the system, and organisational processing functions something like a funnelling process. Ninth, the police supervisory system is not designed prospectively to guide decisions and discretion, but to (a) protect against the claim that something was not done; (b) punish persons after the fact; (c) maintain the appearance of evaluation, if not of evaluational capacity; (d) maintain autonomy among and between units within the system by leaving the principal integrative bases tacit and unspecified (Manning, 1977, Ch. 6).

If one examines the relevance of these ideas to the paramilitary model, they suggest that it is very unlikely that the police could be fully controlled and supervised, given the ecological distribution of the units and their essential invisibility during large parts of the shift. In addition to the fundamental ecological constraint (which the several radio and other communicational channels were meant to overcome, but do not), there are three other reasons why supervisors are in fact unable to supervise closely lower participants. The situations with which the police deal are ambiguous, diverse, subject to multiple interpretations, extended in time and space, and require complex human judgements. The bonds of solidarity between police officers are strong, and grow from their shared exposure to danger, their isolation and conflict with the public. Finally, the police are given enough freedom by supervisors (realistically so) that they often have the power to embarrass them, and to make their supervisors in fact dependent on them for good performances which are not too exposing (see the useful summary of these matters in Jermier and Berkes, 1979). The discretionary possibilities and supervisory ritual multiplies and amplifies the effects of discretion. Discretion is not admitted, and when it is recognised, it is treated as important *only* when other circumstances are changed and not because discretion and non-discretion is valued.

At the very least these bits of information suggest that the paramilitary model of policing mediates between the citizen and the internal survival needs of the organisation, and that the fundamental internal sense-making and processing of information is at least as important as 'demand' measured by such surrogate indices as characteristics of community structure (Lineberry, 1977), or aggregated official statistics such as the crime or arrest rate in a city. The organisation maintains an important degree of control over information, and in a sense the system of information-gathering creates and shapes what it is capable of accepting from the environment. In fact, it is likely that the neat distinction between the environment and the organisation, looked at in this way, is not so neat at all.

The environment and the organisation

The evidence assembled here, albeit of a somewhat miscellaneous character, can be used to reflect on the argument concerning the degree of the citizens' control over policing in Anglo-American societies. If the transformation of calls takes place as suggested in the data from the Midwestern Police Department, then simple distinctions between the environment and the organisation do not appear to be tenable.

The information processing structure of the organisation is in effect a technology. It is often claimed that technology is the defining characteristic of organisations (e.g., Perrow, 1970), while it is also claimed that in the case of people-processing organisations the distinction between technology and organisational structure is difficult to pin down (Manning, in press).   If we grant that at the centre of any organisation is its knowledge technology, and this is certainly true for the police, then the information processing system must be at the centre of the analysis of the environment-organisation relationship. The means by which the organisation applies knowledge to the accomplishment of work tasks, or knowledge technology, is indeterminant in policing. Technology in policing is indeterminant because the tasks that are undertaken are so individualised, the sequencing of tasks is controlled by the lower participants (the officer on the ground), and the 'material' processed by the police is human. People, both managers and citizens, have choice and freedom to do otherwise. It is virtually impossible to measure the 'environment' to which the 'technology' is directed, because they are both rooted in the sense-making, sensate, symbolic-processing human consciousness. Weick, in a series of brilliant arguments, has made this case in the most convincing manner:

> Although one of the central propositions in any evolutionary
> theory concerns the continuing press of the environment on

115

the organism, the precise nature of this environment is never made explicit. This lack of clarity is especially troublesome when we begin to think of human organisations within an evolutionary framework ... information is the commodity processed in human systems, and information retained by the actor may then constrain his subsequent actions. These subtle features of human organising are difficult to fit into the gross portraits of the environment which are associated with evolutionary theory. We need a more explicit statement of what constitutes the environment of an organisation, and we need to be certain that this portrait is consistent with what is known about the ways in which human beings function. Instead of discussing the 'external environment', we will discuss the 'enacted environment'. The phase the 'enacted environment' preserves the crucial distinctions that we wish to make, the most important being that the human *creates* the environment to which the system adapts. The human does not *react* to any environment, he *en*acts to it. It is this enacted environment, and nothing else, that is worked upon by the process of organising. (Weick, 1969, pp.63—64)

We have suggested the symbolic processing of information while examining briefly a police dispatch system. If the ways in which participants perceive, define and act upon the environment, and the ways in which they chunk and decode memories of experience are socially rooted, and to some extent patterned by the segments in the organisation in which they experience organisational activities, then the environment cannot usefully be seen as a single *object.* It must be seen as an entity that *variably* and *phenomenologically* links the organisation and external events. The potential for loose coupling (Weick, 1976) is maintained.

The capacity of the organisation to produce its own coding system by which received messages are encoded and then decoded is enormous. As a result, the organisation has important *independent symbolic and symbolising capacities.* The organisation is a system of signs by which other signs are encoded and stored, hence to be decoded. It is, in effect a crude *semiological* system. Thus, the term enacted environment is a reflexive concept: it refers to what is 'seen' in the external world, but also to the structure by which such seeing is made possible. In a sense, seeing and the seen are two sides of the same system of thought, action and praxis. To separate them is to do a logical injustice. (See Dewey and Bentley, 1949.) Police organisations are differentiated semiotic systems based on information and encoding processes (see Manning, in press).   In other words, it is

116

impossible to separate and measure the organisation and the environment because the perceptions, understandings, beliefs, myths, and enactments of members as much constitutes the environment as it is a reaction to some unchanging object 'out there'. It is as rational to argue that organisations *create* a sense of the environment to which organisational members react to and adjust to over time, as to argue that the environment, working through the proximal influence of technology, creates and sustains the organisation (see Silverman, 1971; Child, 1972; Aldrich and Pfeffer, 1976; Weick, 1976; Manning, in press).

It is difficult to assign credibility to arguments such as those made by Reiss and Bordua, to the effect that the external informational environment has shaped the police. It is perhaps useful to bear in mind the proposition that once one knows the system of rules by which the world is classified by a group, one has discovered the rules or principles of organisation thought to govern both (see Tiryakian, 1978, discussing Durkheim.) The paramilitary model is as much a myth articulating the organisation of the world as it is a model of police operations.

It is furthermore unlikely at present that arguments concerning the patterning effect of information on organisational structure can be proven in the case of the police. (See summaries of these ideas in Lillenfeld, 1979.) For in order to factor out *information*, or a bit of data that alters the probability of the next bit of data, from *meaning*, or the likelihood that such a bit of information, or chunk of it, will alter the tendency to act of the unit receiving the information, one would have to develop not only a number of measures of information within the police, one also would have to engage in the sort of semiotic analysis which has only been suggested in the middle portion of the paper. No conclusions can be drawn about the effectiveness of the police with respect to the environment until the distinctions between the 'environment' and the 'organisation' are made more precisely.

In recent reviews of the effect of the police on crime with special emphasis on technology and its contribution to crime control, it was concluded that there is no firm evidence presently available that police technology reduces crime (Colton, 1978; Manning, in press). This finding is consistent with the other research which has shown the rather marginal impact of the police on crime in any case, given the enormous contribution of such matters as legal constraints, public attitudes, informational limitations, cultural traditions, and the diversity of what is labelled 'crime'. Technology has no invariant meanings, no predictable singular effects, no lasting consequences, and no simple and direct impact on crime. The information approach to policing assumes the determinant centrality of information and information-processing technology on crime control, (e.g., Willmer, 1970). In the United States and to a lesser degree, in the United Kingdom, this approach has adopted not only the notion of a tight coupling obtaining between the police and the environment, it has also assumed a rather tight internal processing capacity for using available information.

The limits on the information approach, suggested in this review, can be illuminated by a final example which compares the capacity of the control tower to pilot communication systems to produce redundancy with that of the police system. Unlike communications between a control tower and aircraft, the level of redundancy in the communication is not facilitated by the context of the message (the standardised units used in communications, and the relatively limited types of situations involved in the landing or taking-off of a plane). The controllers and the pilots can monitor each others' movements by radar, radio and even visually at some times of the day, the number of situations involved is limited and known, the codes are consistently used, and the physical ecological setting is invariant for the given participants. Thus, if this system is an example of high redundancy (see Frick and Sumby, 1952), policing would appear to be a system with relatively low redundancy (high information), which suggests the existence of system-compensation devices such as ritualised response, high individualised discretion, and other attempts to control the message system. These processes, alluded to previously in *Police Work* (1977, ch. 6 and 7), suggest the importance of close analysis of internal processing of information, and caution with regard to making deterministic statements about the environment-organisation interchange, role of the citizen in shaping the police response, and the effectiveness of the police in crime work.

Appendix

Incident codes: eight of the twenty-two main categories*

31 *Homicide/death*

1-3100 Homicide (kill another)
1-3111 Att. suicide in prog.
2-3112 Suicide just happ.
2-3119 Suicide rept.
2-3120 Dead person (nat./acc.)

34 *Assault*

1-3401 FA in prog.
2-3402 FA just happ.
3-3409 FA rept.
1-3412 Shooting just happ.
1-3422 Cutting just happ.
1-3431 Person w/weapon there now
2-3432 Person w/weapon just left
2-3441 Shots H/F now
3-3442 Shots H/F just happ.
4-3449 Shots H/F rept.
1-3451 Kidnapping in prog.
2-3452 Kidnapping just happ.
2-3453 Kidnapping att/just happ.
3-3459 Kidnapping rept.
1-3461 A & B in prog. (no weapon)
4-3469 A & B rept.

35 *Burglary*

1-3501 B & E business in prog.
2-3502 B & E bus. just happ.
3-3503 B & E bus. att/just happ.
3-3509 B & E bus. rept.
1-3511 B & E dwelling in prog.
2-3512 B & E dwell. just happ.
2-3513 B & E dwell. att/just happ.
4-3519 B & E dwelling rept.
1-3531 B & E auto in prog.
3-3532 B & E auto just happ.
4-3539 B & E auto rept.
1-3541 B & E other in prog.
2-3542 B & E other just happ.
3-3543 B & E other att/just happ.

4-3549 B & E other rept.
2-3551 Glass breaking
2-3560 People away/lights on
3-3570 Investigate building
2-3580 Open door
3-3590 Enter w/o permission

37 *Automobiles*

2-3701 UDAA in prog.
2-3702 UDAA just happ.
4-3709 UDAA rept.
3-3711 Tamp.w/auto in prog.
4-3719 Tamp. w/auto rept.
4-3720 Recovered auto.
2-3731 Stripping auto now
3-3740 Investigate auto.
3-3750 One over wheel

39 *Family trouble/domestic violence*

1-3900 FT homicide
1-3901 FT FA in prog.
2-3902 FT FA just happ.
3-3909 FT FA rept.
1-3911 FT shooting J/H
1-3921 FT cutting J/H
1-3931 FT person w/weapon
2-3932 FT person weapon J/L
1-3941 FT fight
1-3951 FT person screaming
1-3961 FT A & B in prog.
3-3969 FT A & B rept.
3-3971 FT MDP in prog.
3-3979 FT MDP rept.
3-3989 FT Spouse abuse law-
injunction/peace bond

82 *Disturbance*

4-8200 Boys
3-8210 Crowd gathering

3-8220 Disorderly gang
3-8230 Fight
3-8250 Landlord/tenant trouble
3-8260 Neighbour trouble
3-8270 Disturbance/trouble
1-8280 Person screaming
3-8290 Noise/radio etc.

84 *Persons*

3-8400 Meet person
3-8401 Meet the bailiff
3-8410 Drunk
2-8420 One down
2-8430 Pt. out wanted person
3-8440 Investigate person
2-8441 Holding person
2-8442 Holding shoplifter
2-8450 Prowler (window peeper)
1-8461 Missing serious (age/mental)
4-8469 Missing rept.
5-8470 VRM
3-8480 Holding missing/runaway

90 *Officers/calls*

1-9000 Officer in trouble
3-9010 Meet officer
4-9020 Call station BZ
5-9021 Call station in-service
4-9030 To station BZ
5-9031 To station in-service
4-9040 Dial BZ
4-9050 Special detail
4-9060 Station security
2-9070 Man the auto.

*The number (1 through 5) in front of the incident code designates the suggested priority of the code. However, runs are dispatched by seriousness, urgency, growth rate, and availability of resources.

References

Aldrich, H., and Pfeffer, J., (1976), 'Environments of organisation', in Inkeles, A., Coleman, J., and Smelser, N., (eds.), *Annual Review of Sociology*, 2, Annual Reviews, Inc., Palo Alto, Calif.

Bercal, T., (1971), 'Calls for police assistance', in Hahn, H., (ed.), *Police in Urban Society*, Sage Publications, Beverley Hills, Calif.

Bieck, W., (1977), *Response Time Analysis: Executive Summary*, Kansas City, Missouri Police Department, Kansas City, Mo.

Bittner, E., (1974), 'A theory of the police', in Jacob, H., (ed.), *The Potential for the Reform of Criminal Justice*, Sage Publications, Beverly Hills, Calif.

Black, D. J., (1971), 'The social organisation of arrest', *Stanford Law Review*, 23, pp. 1087–1111.

Bordua, D., (1968), 'The police', in Sills, D., (ed.), *International Encyclopedia of Social Science*, Free Press, New York.

Cain, M., (1973), *Society and the Policeman's Role*, Routledge and Kegan Paul, London.

Chaiken, J., (1978), 'Deterrent effects of police activities', in Cramer, J. A., (ed.), *Preventing Crime*, Sage Publications, Beverly Hills, Calif.

Chatterton, M., (1973), 'A working paper on the use of resource-charges and practical decision making in peace-keeping', presented at Bristol Seminar on the Sociology of the Police, Bristol University, England.

Child, J., (1972), 'Organisational structure and performance: the role of stragetic choice', *Sociology*, 6, pp. 1–22.

Colton, K. W., (ed.), (1978), *Police Computer Technology*, D. C. Heath, Lexington, Mass.

Cordner, G. W., (1979), 'Police patrol workload studies: a review and critique', unpublished paper, School of Criminal Justice, Michigan State University.

Cumming, E., Cumming, I., and Edell, L., (1965), 'Policeman as philosopher, guide and friend', *Social Problems*, 12, pp. 276–86.

Davis, K. C., (1969), *Discretionary Justice*, University of Illinois Press, Urbana.

Davis, K. C., (1975), *Police Discretion*, West Publishing Company, St Paul.

Dewey, J., and Bentley, A., (1949), *Knowing and the Known*, Beacon Press, Boston.

Frick, F. C., and Sumby, W. M., (1952), 'Control tower language', *Journal of the Acoustical Society of America*, 24, pp. 595–6.

Goffman, E., (1959), *The Presentation of Self in Everyday Life*, Doubleday, New York.

Gouldner, A. W., (1959), 'Organisational analysis', in Merton, R. K., Broom, L., and Cottrell, L. S. Jr., *Sociology Today*, Basic Books, New York.

Henig, J., Lineberry, R. L., and Milner, N., (1977), 'On the inside looking out: police policy and external determinants', unpublished paper, Northwestern University, Reactions to Crime Project, delivered to the annual meeting of the American Political Science Association, Washington, DC, 1977.

Hughes, E. C., (1971), *The Sociological Eye*, Aldine, Chicago.

Jermier, J., and Berkes, L. J., (1979), 'Leader behaviour in a police command bureaucracy: a closer look at the quasi-military model', *Administrative Science Quarterly*, 24, pp. 1—23.

Larson, R. C., Colton, K. W., and Larson, G. C., (1978), 'Evaluation of Phase I implementation of an Automatic Vehicle Monitoring (AVM) System in St Louis', in Colton, K. W., (ed.), *Police Computer Technology*, D. C. Heath, Lexington, Mass.

Lillenfeld, F., (1979), *The Rise of Systems Theory*, Wiley, New York.

Lilly, J. R., (1978), 'What are the police now doing?', *Journal of Police Science and Administration*, 6, pp. 51—60.

Lineberry, P., (1977), *Equality and Urban Policy*, Sage Publications, Beverly Hills, Calif.

McNamara, J., (1967), 'Uncertainties in police work: the relevance of recruits background and training', in Bordua, D. J., (ed.), *The Police*, John Wiley and Sons, New York.

Manning, P. K., (1977), *Police Work: The Social Organisation of Policing*, Massachusetts Institute of Technology Press, Cambridge, Mass.

Manning, P. K., (1979a), 'Semiotics and loose-coupling', unpublished paper, Michigan State University, East Lansing, Mich.

Manning, P. K., (1979b), 'The social control of police work: observations on the occupational culture of policing', in Holdaway, S., (ed.), *British Police*, Edward Arnold, Ltd., London.

Manning, P. K., (in press), 'Crime and technology: the role of scientific research and technology in crime control in National Science Foundation', *The Five Year Outlook for Science and Technology*, vol. III, US Government Printing Office, Washington, DC.

Martin, J., and Wilson, G., (1968), *The Police: A Study in Manpower*, Heinemann Books, London.

Miller, W., (1977), *Cops and Bobbies*, University of Chicago Press, Chicago.

Niederhoffer, A., (1967), *Behind the Shield*, Doubleday Anchor, New York.

O'Connor, R. J., and Gilman, B., (1978), 'The Police role in deterring crime', in Cramer, J. A., (ed.), *Preventing Crime,* Sage Publications, Beverly Hills, Calif.

Pepinsky, M., (1976), 'Police patrolmen's offense-reporting behaviour', *Journal of Research in Crime and Delinquency,* 13, pp. 33-47.

Perrow, C., (1970), *Organisation Analysis,* Brooks/Cole, Belmont, Calif.

Reiss, A. J., Jr., (1971), *The Police and the Public,* Yale University Press, New Haven.

Reiss, A. J., and Bordua, D., (1967), 'Organisation and environment a perspective on the municipal police', in Bordua, D. (ed.), *The Police,* John Wiley and Sons, New York.

Reith, C., (1943), *The Police and the Democratic Ideal,* Oxford University Press, London.

Rubinstein, J., (1973), *City Police,* Farrar, Straus and Giroux, New York.

Selznick, P., (1966), *TVA and the Grass Roots,* Torchbooks, New York.

Silverman, D., (1971), *The Theory of Organisation,* Basic Books, New York.

Tiryakian, E. A., (1978), 'Emile Durkheim', in Bottomore, T., and Nisbet, R., (eds.), *The History of Sociological Analysis,* Basic Books, New York.

Van Maanen, J., (1974), 'Working the street: a developmental view of police behavior', in Jacob, H. (ed.), *The Potential for Reform of Criminal Justice,* Sage Publications, Beverly Hills, Calif.

Webster, J. A., (1973), *The Realities of Police Work,* Kendall-Hunt, Dubuque, Iowa.

Weber, M., (1947), *The Theory of Economic and Social Organisation,* Translation with an Introduction by T. Parsons, The Free Press, Glencoe.

Weick, K., (1969), *The Social Psychology of Organising,* Adison-Wesley, Reading, Mass.

Weick, K., (1976), 'Educational organisations as loosely coupled systems', *Administrative Science Quarterly,* 21, pp. 1–19.

Willmer, M. A. P., (1970), *Crime and Information Theory,* Edinburgh University Press, Edinburgh.

Wilson, J. Q., (1968), *Varieties of Police Behavior,* Harvard University Press, Cambridge, Mass.

Wilson, O. W., and McLaren, R., (1972), *Police Administration,* (3rd ed.), McGraw-Hill, New York.

7 Experiments on police effectiveness: the Dutch experience
D. W. Steenhuis

Introduction

In September 1978 the Dutch Council of Attorneys General announced that 'increasing crime, declining clearance rates and shortages of police manpower necessitate the establishment of priorities in the detection and reporting of offenders'. The Council felt that such an exercise would require close contact between the police and the two authorities to whom they are accountable—public prosecutors and local mayors—and proposed a formal system of 'tripartite consultation'. The Council endorsed the recommendation of an earlier working party that priorities should be established at local level by tripartite consultation between mayors (as heads of local police forces), public prosecutors and local police chiefs. (National priorities were to be settled elsewhere.) The Council defined the scope of this consultation as 'the lasting deliberation between representatives of the Public Prosecutions Department, local government (the mayor) and the police about penal and administrative action in dealing with crimes and their prevention, and about the use of personnel and material resources in that respect'.

In setting these terms of reference for tripartite consultation the Council intended to make it clear that 'the point at issue is the control and eventual reduction of crime to acceptable limits by co-ordinating administrative measures aimed at the maintenance of public order and penal measures'. The local mayor's role in the consultative process was to represent the interests of his community in the maintenance of order; he would also be involved in his role of administrator of the local police force. The police chief would bring to the consultation his practical knowledge of policing, whilst the public prosecutor, representing the interests of justice, would be responsible for the maintenance of law. The Council also made a further recommendation concerning prosecutors' roles in the consultative process—which provides the main focus of this paper. Prosecutors in some areas were to initiate experiments on the detection and referral for prosecution of minor crimes. These experiments would be underpinned and evaluated scientifically, but were not to retard other efforts to find new methods of crime control. As a result of this recommendation, the Research and Documentation Centre (RDC) of the Ministry of Justice was asked to plan a programme of experimental research.

Police research in the Netherlands, unlike the United States, has only constituted a minor part of the total research effort in criminal justice. The prison system, sentencing and the treatment of offenders have been far more thoroughly researched. Only recently has much police research been undertaken; this began on a modest scale, but is now developing more rapidly. As a consequence neither the police authorities nor the police themselves have much awareness of the results of research conducted in the United States. This should be said to draw attention to the current state of development of the Dutch police, which is one stage behind that of the Americans.

Before describing the RDC's research programme it is worth outlining one further aspect of Dutch policing; that is the way in which the police are located within governmental organisation and are accountable to governmental authorities. The position of the Dutch police is somewhere between that of police in the United States, who are subject to considerable political control, and that of British police, who have very much more political autonomy. The following section offers a brief sketch of the Dutch system.

Police, public prosecution and local government

The organisation of the police

The organisation of the police services in the Netherlands is regulated by the Police Act of 1957, under which the police are divided into two categories. One is the national 'State Police Corps' covering the smaller municipalities, which total 736 and have a combined population of about five million people. The Minister of Justice is responsible for the internal organisation and general management of this Corps, which has a current strength of about 8,000 men. The other is the municipal police, consisting of 130 separate municipal corps, which cover the larger municipalities, with an aggregate population of about eight million. The mayor of each municipality is formal head of the local police, and the strength and composition of each municipal corps is determined by the Minister of Home Affairs. Municipal corps comprise 16,000 men in all.

The Mayor's Authority

The duties of the police under the Police Act are 'to maintain the legal order and give assistance to those in need of it, in subordination to the competent authorities and according to the rules of law'. From this Act three specific tasks are usually deduced:

(i)   maintaining public order (as in demonstrations);
(ii) law enforcement (in concrete form: crime prevention and criminal investigation);
(iii) assisting people who need help.

The mayor is responsible for the activities of the police, be it national or municipal, in relation to the first of these tasks, the maintenance of public order. As the chairman of the Municipal Executive he is responsible for the decisions made by this Executive to the Municipal Council, and thus the Council has within its remit issues of local policy regarding this aspect of policing.

The Public Prosecution Department

Criminal proceedings in the Netherlands may only be instituted by the Department of Public Prosecutions as a representative of the State in the courts. The Department consists of about 180 Public Prosecutors, and is structured hierarchically: Public Prosecutors work under the supervision of Chief Public Prosecutors (responsible for geographical regions), who in turn are subject to Attorneys General at the Courts of Appeal for those regions. They all are responsible to the Minister of Justice, who however, 'reigns with velvet gloves' and only very rarely concerns himself with the details of a specific case. Prosecutors have extensive discretion in deciding whether or not to prosecute; Dutch law recognises the principle of 'expedience' as distinct from the principle of 'legality'. In countries which follow the 'legality principle'—West Germany, for example—the prosecutor is expected to prosecute the cases made known to him by the police. But in the Netherlands a prosecutor is free not to prosecute even when there is sufficient evidence and even if the victim requests a prosecution. (The victim however can appeal against the prosecutor's decision at the Court of Appeal.) Under Dutch criminal law, a case can be dismissed 'in the common interest'. As a result of its organisational structure and prosecutorial discretion, the entire Department of Public Prosecution enjoys a considerable degree of autonomy. During the last two decades this prosecutorial discretion has been significantly extended. In 1975 the criterion 'why not prosecute?' was for the first time officially changed to 'why prosecute?'. Consequently, more cases (where sufficient evidence is available) are now dismissed than prosecuted, and similarly there is a greater use of conditional discharges. The extension of prosecutorial discretion created not just greater opportunities to formulate criminal policy but, rather, an urgent need for such policy. The Department of Public Prosecution soon learned that in order to institute criminal policy successfully, some control was needed over the law enforcement activities of the police, as 'gatekeepers' of the prosecution system. The Department has always had formal authority to exert such control since, in addition to its prosecutorial responsibilities, it has both a legal duty for the maintenance of law, and powers to supervise police investigative activities. Until recently this authority was hardly exercised; prosecutors concentrated on the processing of cases rather than the formulation of criminal policy. However the situation has changed considerably over the last few years, and criminal policy has become a major topic on the Department's agenda. It is increasingly realised that the establishment of such a policy can only successfully be achieved in close co-operation with the police. This is not always easy, as the police are unaccustomed to such attention from prosecutors and tend to resist what they regard as an encroachment on their own territory.

This is where the experiments come in: the prosecutors hope to use them as a lever to regain their control over the police. The experiments provide prosecutors both with a rationale for convening meetings as part of the tripartite consultative process, and with concrete plans to discuss at these meetings. Of course successful tripartite consultation is a prerequisite for the success of the experiments: the co-operation of the police is essential, and as crime and crime prevention overlap with the mayor's sphere of responsibility, public order, he must also be consulted.

The original RDC research programme

As mentioned above, the original goal of the research was to evaluate the effect on crime levels of various policies relating to investigation and referral for prosecution. Criminal investigation departments provided the starting point for the programme, and two approaches to improving effectiveness were identified—intensifying or redistributing investigative resources, and mounting publicity campaigns.

Under the first approach, five experiments were proposed:

1 Setting up and evaluating a 'strike force'—a specialised detective unit dealing with a specific type of offence.
2 Setting priorities for the investigation of specific types of

offences (necessarily resulting in lower priorities for other types of offences) and evaluating the consequences.
3 Setting up and evaluating a team policing scheme.
4 Transferring investigative activities to patrol departments, and evaluating the consequences.
5 Instituting and evaluating new patrolling methods.

Under the second approach, only one experiment was in fact proposed—the evaluation of a large scale publicity campaign—leaving patrol and investigation activities unchanged. It was thought that this would probably consist of a campaign to improve the quantity and quality of crime-reporting by the public or to encourage the public to take physical security measures against burglary.

From the beginning it was envisaged that experiments would be restricted to minor offences only. Within this category a further choice had to be made because only those offences committed fairly frequently and showing a rather stable pattern were considered to be suited. Offences considered, for example were: pickpocketing, minor burglaries, theft from cars and vandalism.

It was considered that the experiments in whatever form should cover at least two large cities, two medium sized towns and two smaller ones. Different districts in each city would serve as experimental and control areas; in the case of the medium sized and small towns one town would be the 'experimental town', the other being its control.

Victim surveys were envisaged as the main instrument for evaluating the experiments. Three main criteria would be used in assessing the outcome of the experiments:

(i)   the number of offences actually committed;
(ii) the reporting behaviour of the victim;
(iii) citizen attitudes towards police performance.

The victim surveys would also establish the level of a public awareness about the experiments.

Attempts to implement the original programme

Once the decision to go ahead with the experiments had been taken by the Attorneys General, agreement to them had to be secured as part of the tripartite consultative process. The first round of negotiations proved no problem. The Attorneys General instructed the relevant Chief Public Prosecutors to put the proposals to their mayors and police chiefs; six tripartite meetings were held, at which researchers from RDC were also present. Agreement in principle was reached at all six meetings; it was decided that provision for additional police manpower for the experiments would be made, and that researchers and police should undertake further discussions about the details of the research.

Problems developed in this second round of negotiations. Several police forces felt that the experiments would be of no value to them. They believed that devoting more resources to the detection of specific offences would improve the detection rates for those offences, but at the end of the day, when the experiments were completed and the additional resources withdrawn, they would be no better off. It was explained that the aim of the experiments was to discover more efficient ways of using available resources, but this argument was only really accepted for the experiments concerned with crime prevention. It was also found that the design of the experiments concerned with investigative methods was invalidated by the fact that in most forces both CID and patrol officers undertook detective work. In particular this limited the value of the experiment in which investigative work was to be transferred to patrol officers. Finally, the police in several areas felt that minor crimes did not constitute a problem for them, and that the experiments were thus irrelevant.

Thus the first research programme had proved too limited to meet the requirements of the police and it was agreed that the RDC would prepare a fresh research plan which again would be discussed with the police.

By the time that negotiations had reached this stage, the RDC had completed a literature survey of American research studies. This concentrated on recent work such as the Rand Study of criminal investigation (Greenwood and Petersilia, 1975), the evaluation of the Rochester system (Bloch and Bell, 1976) and several studies of team policing (e.g., Schwarz and Clarren, 1977). The picture emerging from these studies is now a familiar one, (see, for example, George Kelling's trenchant summary, 1978), and its details need not be repeated here. It is sufficient to say that the first programme of research was based on an inadequate model of policing, and that we had to broaden the scope of the experiments not simply to accommodate the police, but also to take into account the findings of this body of American research.

One further factor had to be taken into account in preparing a second programme of research. It will be remembered that the initiative for the experiments came from the Council of Attorneys General and that a secondary objective in proposing them was to stimulate tripartite consultation between Chief Public Prosecutors, the mayors in their regions and the chiefs of police. The tripartite consultative process was reviewed at a conference attended by Attorneys General, Chief Public Prosecutors and senior officials of the Ministry of Justice. The outcome of this review could in my opinion be a major hindrance to successful execution of criminal policy because the prosecutors seemed apprehensive of the consequences of sharing their burden of responsibility for the law-enforcement activities of the police with their partners in the triangle.

Rethinking the programme

These three sets of factors—police resistance, the findings of American research, and problems in the tripartite consultative process—all had their impact on the development of the second research programme. Most salient, perhaps, were the American research findings, and it should be emphasised that the model of policing which informed the original research programme had to be modified. The main conclusion which we drew from the American research was that criminal investigation does not offer the most promising avenue for improving police effectiveness. The Rand and Rochester studies have clearly demonstrated that 'the role played by investigation in crime solution is overrated', and they suggest 'means of using patrol officers to improve investigative effectiveness' (Kelling, 1978). Further support for this approach is to be found in the Kansas City Preventive Patrolling Experiment, which questioned the value of routine patrol, the main activity in which patrol officers at present engage, (Kelling, et al., 1974). But if patrol officers are to be used successfully as a means of improving investigative effectiveness, certain preconditions have to be met. The first of these is the improvement of relations between the police and the public (Greenwood and Petersilia, 1975), without which no improvement in police effectiveness can be achieved. Not only do the police rely on the public to provide information essential to detection; public support is also essential if police intervention is to be kept to a minimum—arguably the hallmark of successful policing.

This argument needs expansion: I believe that it is foolish to have high expectations of police effectiveness in a society which lacks a coherent and consistent commitment to its laws. For example, the police cannot hope to make any impact on drunken driving in a society where the use of alcohol has become an integral part of social life, its consumption grossly stimulated by the media and its abuse widely accepted as an inevitable consequence of such a society. However simple this observation may seem, it is often over-looked in disucssions of police function.

130

The police should make it very clear to their authorities and to the public that any effort to upgrade police effectiveness is bound to fail if there is not what might be called *continuity of enforcement*. Enforcement in this sense embraces not only police activity, but the preventive measures taken by public authorities and private individuals. The police cannot make any impact on crime whilst citizens fail to take care of their own physical safety and to protect their homes and other property against crime; they cannot operate effectively whilst public authorities refuse to consider even the most obvious crime prevention measures.

It will not be easy to introduce this new concept of policing—to achieve continuity of enforcement. But the attempt must be made, as in my view, it is the only way to break the vicious circle of mutual discontent and alienation which exists between the police and the public. The problems encountered in the process must be solved not by the police alone, but by all members of the triangle—police, mayors and prosecutors—as well as, of course, by the public themselves. Only in this way can continuity of enforcement be achieved.

It will require a great deal of effort on the part of the police and their authorities to mobilise the public in this joint venture: as things stand, the public cannot be expected to make the first move. People see no continuity of enforcement, and feel that the police and the authorities have failed to discharge their responsibilities for crime control (Junger-Tas, 1975). They see the police reluctant to respond to calls for assistance; they believe that the detection rate is too low; that the police refer too few cases to the prosecutors; that the prosecutors too rarely act on these referrals; that there is no co-ordination of police and prosecution policies, and so on. This disenchantment will prove a very severe obstacle to achieving public co-operation. It can be overcome if the police show a genuine preparedness to respond to public feeling and public fear or crime. This will involve not only improvements in investigative techniques and strategies aimed at reducing fear of crime (by distinguishing between myth about crime and reality), but active community based crime prevention is also required—'pro-active policing' as advocated by Alderson (1978).

It is one thing to outline a new approach to policing, but quite another to implement even a few of its features in an experimental research programme. The Dutch police, with a few exceptions, subscribe to the policing model implicit in our original programme, and only very recently have new concepts of policing received any attention (Projectgroep Organisatie Structuren, 1977). Preventive patrolling and fast response to calls for police assistance are still regarded as effective strategies of crime control, and little is known about

131

approaches such as crime prevention through environmental design (Newman, 1972) and team policing. So it was an uphill task to convert police, mayors and prosecutors to the new approach.

In drawing up our second programme of research we made two main shifts of emphasis. The experiments focused on patrol officers rather than the CID; and rather than viewing the police as the only agents of social control, we saw the public as a major resource for crime prevention. We also tried to widen the concept of crime prevention from physical 'locks and bolts' intervention (which has considerable support in the Netherlands) to social prevention—the 'primary prevention' of John Alderson. These shifts of emphasis constitute in effect a change in the ultimate objectives of the experiments. The original programme was intended to generate effective methods of dealing with specific, local, crime problems; the revised version was aimed at the introduction of a new style of policing, which would combat minor crime as a whole.

The shape of the new programme was also affected by methodological considerations. More detailed examination of the towns and cities in which the research was to be set revealed that control and experimental areas were not sufficiently comparable for reliable evaluation. Crime rates were also very low, and showed considerable fluctuations over time; it would have proved difficult to differentiate between changes in crime levels attributable to the experiments and those which were simply random fluctuations. So we decided to drop paired comparison as an experimental design, and to use data from the National Victim Survey to provide experimental control. (The RDC carries out a yearly victim survey at a national level, with sample size of 10,000.) It was thus no longer necessary to use all six research settings, and as it happens, two towns withdrew from the research programme, on the grounds that they did not have a crime problem.

Our shift of emphasis also affected the secondary objective of the research programme—to stimulate tripartite consultation. The terms of reference of the consultative process were originally to agree policies about detection and prosecution. With the introduction of the new style of policing these were broadened to include the coordination of broad based crime preventive measures.

Research under the second programme

Utrecht: team policing

In Utrecht, the fourth largest city in the Netherlands, the entire police corps is being reorganised along team policing lines, with a planned completion date in 1980. As part of the project a number of different crime prevention schemes will be undertaken.

It has been agreed that the Utrecht Police will themselves evaluate internal aspects of the reorganisation (for example, job satisfaction of personnel) and that the RDC will carry out external evaluation. We aim to assess the effectiveness of team policing in reducing both crime and the fear of crime and in improving relations between the police and the public. A survey of public attitudes to the police was carried out in 1979, before team policing was implemented, and a follow-up survey will be done in 1981. Research findings will be reported in 1982.

Utrecht: improving investigative efficiency

With growing concern in Utrecht about increases in the level of burglary and decreases in burglaries cleared up it was decided to mount a 'burglary project', which began at the end of 1978.

A burglary squad has been set up, consisting of a sergeant, acting as co-ordinator, six detectives (who are relieved of all normal duties), eight patrol officers, and administrative personnel. The patrol officers (two from each of Utrecht's four geographical divisions) rotate on a weekly basis. If required, the team receives assistance from the CID and from the State Police. The team co-ordinator, rather than individual detectives, decides whether a case warrants investigation, on the basis of information available at the time of discovery of the crime. Administrative procedures have been stream-lined, so that detectives have more time for genuine investigative work. As the team are in daily contact with each other, there is a greater exchange of information between detectives, and in addition there has been a restructuring of information obtained from the CID. The project's primary goals are to achieve an increased detection rate for burglary and theft with a reduced investment of manpower, and to get to grips with organised crime. Secondary goals are to increase detectives' job satisfaction and to improve the integration of patrol and investigation departments.

The RDC are evaluating the project. Data will be collected from police and court records covering the six-month periods either side of the start of the project, and detection 'clear-up' rates and methods of detection will be compared. Additional information will be coll-ected (by interview and other means) to document the implementa-tion of the project and to assess the attitudes of participants. Find-ings should be reported early in 1980.

The Hague

The RDC is involved in a project initiated by The Hague Police, which began in March 1979. It will run for six months initially, and then be reviewed. The project setting is a district of The Hague built just after the last war, consisting mainly of low-rise flats, with a population of 20,000, many of whom are elderly. Project goals are to reduce levels of burglary, to reduce fear of burglary and to improve the burglary detection rate. As improved police/public relations are seen as a precondition for achieving these goals, considerable effort is being invested in primary preventive measures; these include the setting up of a mutual aid project for old people (in conjunction with welfare agencies), improving playground facilities, and supporting tenants in negotiations for better external lighting and improved physical security in their homes.

The project is being run by a team of eight patrol officers and two detectives, under the supervision of a sergeant and a chief inspector. The police crime prevention department is also closely involved. Evaluation is being carried out by a researcher from The Hague Police, guided by a steering committee on which the RDC are represented. A second district, comparable to the project setting, has been selected to provide experimental control. The RDC has been further involved in that it conducted a victim survey at the start of the project; this was both to provide a baseline of burglary levels, and to assist at the project's planning stage by defining the nature and extent of the problem.

Hoogeveen

An experiment set in Hoogeveen is scheduled to begin in 1980 and will last a year. This will focus on burglaries, thefts from cars and vandalism, and will aim to reduce levels of crime and fear of crime, to improve relations between police and public, and to increase the public's preparedness to report crimes to the police. Selective preventive patrolling will be undertaken in vulnerable locations, and crime prevention information will be disseminated at schools and neighbourhood meetings, and via the media.

A sample of the population will be interviewed before and after the experiment and attitudes towards crime and the police and responses to the experiment will be assessed. Data from police records and other sources (such as local authority maintenance departments and shopkeepers' associations) will be used to assess the experiment's impact on levels of crime. Qualitative information will be collected by interview from participants in the experiment.

Amsterdam and Leiden

Experiments are planned for Amsterdam and Leiden, to begin at the end of 1979. The experiments will have the same design and objectives as that in The Hague, except that they will focus not only on burglary but also on theft from cars and vandalism. The experiments will be evaluated at their conclusion and after a further period of a year, using the same methods as in the Hoogeveen experiment.

Conclusion

The new concept of policing discussed above has been severely criticised both on grounds of feasibility and desirability (de Lange, 1978). As far as feasibility is concerned the main issue is whether a strong integration of police and public can be achieved in modern western society. As for desirability it is open to question whether the police should play the role assigned to them in the new approach. There are a great number of possible disadvantages. Rather than deal at length with this criticism, I shall try to assess how these drawbacks might impinge on the experiments.

Naturally Dutch society displays to a certain extent the features of a modern industralised welfare state, but in many aspects it differs considerably from the norm. All these differences in my view make the chances of successful introduction of the experiments greater in the Netherlands than perhaps in any other European countries.

First, administration in Holland has always been rather decentralised, and the citizen feels strong ties with local government. Secondly, the country has a strong and long standing anti-authoritarian tradition which may mean that there is greater scope for improved co-operation between the public and the police. Moreover, the Dutch seem to have a fairly strong inclination to moralise, which may both explain and stimulate informal social control in this country.

But at the same time they also have a high level of tolerance for deviant behaviour. This perhaps is one of the main explanations for the very lenient sentencing policy in the Netherlands and the very humane penal system.

Finally, the level of crime in Holland is low in comparison with almost any other European country. This factor may in one way or another be related to the other ones.

Of course apparently favourable conditions for the introduction of change do not automatically justify that change. A feasible concept is not necessarily a good one. However, those who do not agree with the new approach should realise the lack of acceptable alternatives. This could stimulate the acceptance of the new one, even taking its disadvantages into account. I do not consider these disadvantages insuperable, however.

The criticism implicit in Manning's (1977) book *Police Work* that too close a relation between the public and the police may prevent the police from playing their ritual role, i.e., representing Authority, does not seem appropriate to the Netherlands. The public do not expect the police to behave in an authoritarian manner. On the contrary, if the police operate in this way they would soon lose goodwill. A second disadvantage mentioned by Banton (1964) that in a close relationship with the public, the police might lose their impartiality, is not specific to the new concept of policing. There is no evidence that in the present model the same problem could not arise. A third objection put forward by Kuitenbrouwer (1978) seems to be of greater importance. He states that a policeman can be involved in role conflict if he is tempted to use in law enforcement information which has been gathered in a 'horizontal' relation based on the co-operation model (Kuitenbrouwer, 1978). This objection carries considerable weight when, as in the Netherlands, police data bases are largely automatised. But as far as I can see, the number of these conflict situations will remain fairly limited. There is simply no need for the police to gather or to use this kind of 'criminal' information against the large majority of citizens providing such information. Conflicts of this sort will be even rarer if the new concept of policing becomes well established. For then the police will no longer need this kind of information to solve minor crimes, as they would only be dealt with in a proactive or preventive way. As far as any repression is exercised this is not 'offender-oriented' but 'phenomenon-oriented'. Moreover, it seems to me that ordinary citizens do not identify very much with offenders even at present, and will have no problem in providing this kind of information. At present, their refusal to co-operate with the police stems not from feelings of solidarity with the offender but from negative experiences in their contact with the police and disillusion with police performance.

In the new situation this identification will be even smaller as the public will have been taught to perceive minor crime as a social rather than as a crime problem, thus enlarging society's 'crime tolerance'. What remains is major crime and the perpetrators of that can make no appeal whatsoever to the understanding of let alone identification from, the general public. Of course, this may enhance stigmatisation of that group of criminals but that, as I see it, may be the price to be paid for 'decriminalisation' of petty crime. Besides, this stigma also exists at the present, but extends to a far larger group of offenders.

There is one more advantage of the new concept of policing. If things work out well the investigation branch will save time that can be used not only in trying to solve major crimes but also in widening the scope of police attention, for example, to economic and ecological crime in co-operation with the special police branches working in those fields. Finally, there is one more general factor, which may prevent the police from becoming involved in role conflict. This is the way in which Dutch police forces are doubly accountable to the mayor on the one hand and to the prosecutor on the other. This is not to say that all problems mentioned before can be overcome in the Netherlands, but that the 'triangle' may be a suitable forum for the discussion and identification of solutions. Certainly there is no guarantee that the new concept can be successfully introduced in the Netherlands. Neither is research the only way to familiarise the police with it. Successful implementation of the concept can in the long run only be achieved if police education and police organisation are thoroughly overhauled.

Police education in the Netherlands is scheduled to be revised in due time. Although the aims of this adjustment are not primarily based on the ideas underlying the new concept, some elements of it no doubt will play a major role in the discussion, viz, a better social training of the police officer.

As for organisation, it has to be seen to what extent likely changes (for example, the combining of the national and the municipal police into a single force) will impede or assist introduction of the new approach.

It is my conviction that introduction of the new model, even in the fairly favourable conditions in the Netherlands, will require a great deal of enthusiasm, imagination and idealism—but also an awareness of practicalities. Thus we have not undertaken all the experiments at the same level but have varied their design from the modest (Amsterdam, Leiden) to the very ambitious (Utrecht), and their application from small cities (Hoogeveen) to larger ones (Amsterdam). Time will tell which is the best road forward.

Acknowledgement

Thanks are due to Drs O. R. de Lange and W. M. Been for their assistance.

References

Alderson, J., (1977), *From Resources to Ideas*, Devon and Cornwall Constabulary, Exeter.

Banton, M., (1964), *The Policeman in the Community*, Tavistock, London.

Bloch, P. B., and Bell, J., (1976), *Managing Investigations: the Rochester System*, Police Foundation, Washington, DC.

Greenwood, P. W., and Petersilia, J., (1975), *The Criminal Investigation Process, Volume I: Summary and Policy Implications*, The Rand Corporation, Santa Monica, Calif.

Kelling, G. L., Pate, T., Dieckman, D., and Brown, C. E., (1974), *The Kansas City Preventive Patrol Experiment: a Summary Report*, Police Foundation, Washington, DC.

Kelling, G. L., (1978), 'Police field services and crime: the presumed effects of a capacity', *Crime and Delinquency*, 2, pp. 173—84.

Kuitenbrouwer, F., (1978), 'Dualisme en verzelfstandiging', *Nederlandse Gemeente*, 7, pp. 75—90.

Lange, O. R. de, (1978), 'Preventie, politie en burgerij', *Justitiele Verkenningen*, 8, pp. 3—28.

Manning, P. K., (1977), *Police Work: The Social Organisation of Policing*, The MIT Press, London.

Newman, O., (1972), *Defensible Space: People and Design in the Violent City*, Architectural Press, London.

Junger-Tas, J., (1978), *Relatie tussen de Primaire Politie-opleiding en de Politie-praktijk, Eindrapport*, Wetenschappelijk Onderzoek en Documentatie Centrum, s-Gravenhage.

Projectgroep Organisatie Structuren (1977), *Politie in Verandering: een Voorlopig Theoretisch Model*, Ministerie van Binnenlandse Zaken, s-Gravenhage.

Schwartz, A. L., and Clarren, S. N., (1977), *The Cincinnati Team Policing Experiment: a Summary Report*, Police Foundation, Washington, DC.

8 Responsibility, competence and police effectiveness in crime control

Peter Engstad and John L. Evans[1]

Introduction

The effectiveness of the police in dealing with crime in Canada and the United States has typically been examined empirically from one of three perspectives: macro-analyses of the effect of police resources on crime occurrence (Wilson and Boland, 1977; Mehay, 1978); analyses of such police functions as patrol (Kelling, et al., 1974) and criminal investigation (Greenwood and Petersilia, 1975); and analyses of police crime prevention programmes such as 'operation identification' (Meuser, 1976; Chaiken, et al., 1975).

While recognising their immense contribution to the rapidly growing literature on policing, these and related studies provide inconclusive results regarding police effectiveness in controlling crime (Chaiken, 1978), a meagre list of constructive suggestions for achieving greater police effectiveness (Henig, et al., 1977), and ambiguous implications for the development of criminal justice policy (Banton, 1978).

A fourth perspective, referred to as 'crime specific' (Wilson, 1975) or 'situational' (Home Office, 1979), in which enforcement and prevention policies and strategies derive from a detailed analysis of how particular crimes are carried out, appears to be a more promising point of departure (Letkeman, 1973; Reppetto, 1974, Clarke, 1977; Cirel, et al., 1977; Waller and Okihiro, 1978; Home Office, 1979; Mayhew, et al., 1979). By combining this perspective with a consideration of the concept of responsibility, we will illustrate how research focusing on specific crimes, on the locus of responsibility for the control of specific types of crime, and on the competence of citizens, individually and collectively, to control specific crime occurrences, is likely to generate constructive suggestions for improving police effectiveness, police management, and criminal justice policy.

While this perspective could be profitably applied to the full range of problems faced by the police (Goldstein, 1979), in this paper we will restrict our attention to its application to crime control.

Focus on crime

Recent experience strongly suggests that crime control strategies, incorporating both law enforcement and the prevention of specific offences, should begin with the identification of the nature, extent, and salience of crime problems in a particular community and a detailed examination of how specific criminal acts are carried out (Wilson, 1975; Farmer, 1976; Home Office, 1979; and Goldstein, 1979). This view is commonly espoused and the police have developed both enforcement and crime prevention strategies appropriate to particular offences or classes of offences. Nonetheless, the full potential of this approach has seldom been realised in practice since both police and citizens have generally accepted the view that crime control was, nearly exclusively, the responsibility of the police (Kelly, 1965). Thus, crime problems have typically been analysed and 'crime attack' strategies (Wilson, 1975) formulated without a careful questioning of who in the community was responsible, to what extent, for the existence or control of specific crimes, thus restricting the search for alternative responses to crime problems.

The locus of responsibility for crime control

The shift towards the police and its consequences

Since Sir Robert Peel established the Metropolitan Police in 1829 (Critchley, 1967), society has become increasingly complex and increasingly legalistic. The evolution of social and legal institutions has been accompanied by a gradual shifting of responsibility for crime control (and for the 'handling' of a vast array of social problems), from citizens to the police (Murphy, 1974; Goldstein, 1979). The police have generally welcomed the growth of their sphere of responsibility and concomitant increase in their powers (Manning, 1971), whether acquired by default, through active lobbying or through legislative acts. Correspondingly, citizens appear to have been willing to relinquish responsibility for crime control (National Advisory Commission, 1973).

This shift in responsibility from the citizenry to the police has been accompanied by a shift in expectations with regard to their respective roles and competence as crime control agents. Here again, police have accepted increasing levels of public expectation. Indeed, the police have greatly overestimated the extent to which they could control crime (Murphy, 1974) and in so doing, have greatly inflated public expectations. Moreover, raising citizens' expectations in regard to the role and competence of the police has had the effect of reinforcing citizens' acceptance of a diminished role and declining competence in crime control.

Having urged acceptance of the view that, given enough resources, the police could effectively control crime, it is now apparent that despite massive increases in police personnel and equipment, the magnitude and seriousness of the crime problem has not abated (Kelling, 1978; Heywood, 1979a, b). Indeed, the argument that more police with better equipment, responding ever more rapidly to calls, will effectively control crime has been discredited in the eyes of a growing number of police administrators and students of policing (Murphy, 1974; Wilson, 1976; Manning, 1977; Krajick, 1978; Clarke and Heal, 1979).

Numerous reasons have been advanced to explain why gains in police resources and increases in efficiency have not been translated into increased police effectiveness in crime control. Principal among these is the view that the police have directed their resources toward improving the traditional means by which police services are delivered, and have paid insufficient attention to the substantive outcome of police practice on the problems they are called upon to handle (Goldstein, 1979). Other authors have attributed the apparent lack of police effectiveness in crime control to the numerous underlying 'causes' of crime over which legislators and the police have virtually no control (Coates, 1974); to the fact that as much as 60 per cent of serious crime occurs in private places which are ordinarily inaccessible to the police (Farmer, 1976); to the failures of the courts and correctional system; to exponential increases in opportunity for crime; and to the existence of the tremendous volume of non-violent property crime which occupies an enormous amount of police resources but which the police, by themselves, have little hope of controlling (Heywood, 1979a; 1979b; Grant, 1979). Finally, in addition to being a serious social concern, 'crime is a source of fun, a means of profit, a source of occupation, and a mainstay of entertainment' (Coates, 1974).

It is clear that the ability of the police to control crime is, at best, limited (Kelling, 1979). Moreover, while the reasons given for the apparent failure of increased police resources to produce commensurate reductions in crime are plausible, and research which would inform the various arguments would no doubt be interesting, establishing their relative merits may be academic, since continued rapid growth in police resources is unlikely.

The shift towards the community and its implications

The developments outlined above, together with increasing demands for fiscal, legal, and social accountability; changes in the economic, social, and demographic characteristics of communities; advances in technology and management philosophy; and challenges to traditional police beliefs and time-honoured practices; are having an unsettling influence on the institution of policing, and appear to be provoking, in Canada and in other Western societies, a re-examination of the nature and extent of police services and the methods of their delivery.

This re-examination has taken a number of forms but the most significant seems to be directed towards breaking down the barriers separating the community and the police. As Parkinson (1977, p. 31) noted in his study of the police and community services project in Vancouver, BC:

> Police departments throughout North America have begun to move towards various forms of 'community policing' programs in which they attempt to redefine their own role in the community, to establish new and more helpful relationships with the community, and to act as catalysts to involve other professionals and citizens in sharing responsibility for things which have been seen as problems for the police alone ... We are going to see growing acceptance by communities that social and economic ills are indeed community problems and to hold the police accountable for the level of crime is totally illogical.

Community policing is likely to have its most significant impact where the police make a conscious attempt to shift the locus of responsibility for crime control to the community. In contrast to the view that police effectiveness in controlling crime would be greatly enhanced if more resources were available, if police powers were enhanced, and if the courts were less lenient, we think the most significant advances in the ability of the police and communities to control crime are likely to arise out of a fundamental reallocation of responsibility for crime control and a concomitant restructuring of the mutual expectations of the police and the public. This optimistic forecast is based on a broader conception and application of the concept of responsibility than is commonly reflected in the literature or in practice.

The concept of responsibility

In Western societies citizens have a responsibility, to themselves and others, to take reasonable precautions to prevent the commission of crimes. To fail to do so is to abrogate a clear social duty and to contribute, however unwittingly, to the generation of crime problems in the community. This conception of responsibility is rooted in our moral and legal traditions. Specific circumstances in which the citizen is bound or empowered to aid the police are usually incorporated in Criminal Codes (Canada, Revised Statutes, 1970). In addition, specific instances in which citizens are obliged to take positive action to prevent the commission of a crime (Oakland Municipal Code, 1969) or preserve the public peace (Ontario, Revised Statutes, 1974) can be found in legal statutes.

In the literature, and less commonly in practice, this moral dictum and its legislative corollaries are usually interpreted to mean that citizens have a duty to take reasonable precautions to protect their personal safety and the security of their property. Or, phrased slightly differently, they have a duty, up to their level of competence, to reduce opportunities for crime.

While few would disagree with these statements, the gradual transference of responsibility for crime control from the citizen to the police has robbed them of their meaning. However, if we begin with the question 'How ought the community be organised to control crime?', thus making the assignment of responsibility for crime control problematic, it is possible to avoid being bound conceptually by the traditional view that the police are responsible and therefore accountable for crime control. The concept of responsibility then provides a basis for examining key aspects of the role and function of the police, as well as for answering practical questions relating to police and community effectiveness in crime control.

The concept of responsibility is a particularly appropriate vehicle for addressing these questions since it requires that the following issues also be considered:

1   It provokes an examination of those factors in the environment which are conducive to crime occurrence, together with an examination of who, individually or collectively, is contributing to the generation of crime problems in the community by creating opportunities for crime or by failing to take reasonable actions to limit opportunities for crime;

2   It requires consideration of the extent to which situational inducements and environmental opportunities for crime can be reduced, together with an assessment of the extent to which those contributing to the existence of crime problems could reasonably

be held responsible for their control;

3   It requires that attention be directed toward the full range of social units (the police, individuals, and assorted agencies and institutions) which have or could acquire competence in crime control, since responsibility for crime control cannot be meaningfully assigned if the individual or organisation to whom responsibility is being entrusted lacks present or potential competence to reduce the crime problem;

4   It requires explicit consideration of the negotiation processes through which changes in the locus of responsibility for crime control are to be affected, since responsibility must be accepted before it constitutes a basis for action. Moreover, a reassignment of responsibility for crime control is much more likely to be effective in those instances where some method is established for securing accountability; and

5   It requires, at the outset, a thorough examination of how specific crimes are carried out, since the determination of responsibility for crime occurrence,[2] responsibility for crime control, competence to control crime, the bases for negotiating the assignment or transfer of responsibility for crime control, and the means for ensuring accountability cannot be determined in the abstract, but only in respect to very specific crime occurrences.

Having taken the position that the most significant advances in policing as an institution, as well as in the effectiveness of the police and communities to control crime, are likely to arise out of a fundamental re-examination of the assignment of responsibility for crime control, and having established the linkage between the concept of responsibility and crime specific analyses, the remainder of this paper is devoted to an examination of the implications of this perspective for the police, for research, and for the development of criminal justice policy.

Implications for the police

In this section we present and discuss two cases which illustrate how the theoretical discussion of responsibility outlined above can be applied in an effort to affect a more appropriate allocation of responsibility for crime control and to develop optimally efficient and effective crime control strategies. In addition, we briefly consider how this perspective contributes to a more realistic view of the ability of the police to control crime, to closer ties between the police and the community they serve, to a more equal balance between the law enforcement and crime prevention functions of the police, and to changes in the organisation and management of policing as an institution.

Consider the following case studies:

Case I[3]

A constable noted, over a period of time, that the police had responded to an unusually large number of calls for service at one of two virtually identical high-density apartment buildings in his zone. These frequent calls for service, which placed a strain on police resources, related primarily to vandalism, noise, petty theft, and related infractions.

The constable confirmed his observation by reviewing dispatch records and discussed the situation with his colleagues and his supervisor. Since it was commonly understood in his department that every effort should be made to reduce the use of police resources to handle crimes and other problems which were well within the competence of others within the community to deal with, the constable and his supervisor suggested to the Chief Constable that a more detailed examination of the problem be undertaken in order to determine whether or not alternative solutions to the problem might be available.

Since the police department was small and had a minimal research capacity, graduate students from a university in a near-by community were encouraged by the Chief Constable to undertake a study of the problem and to suggest possible explanations as to why only one of the adjacent buildings was generating a high incidence of calls for service. The students reported that the only significant difference they could find between the two buildings and their occupants was the quality of management. The building that generated the calls for service had a tenant-manager who was negligent in cleaning and making repairs, didn't make or enforce rules regarding behaviour in the building, and showed little regard either for the building or its tenants. The adjacent building, from which very few calls for police service originated, was neat, clean and in good repair. The tenant-manager made and enforced rules governing conduct in the building and was well liked by the tenants.

With this information in hand, the Chief Constable visited the delinquent manager and discussed the responsibility of building managers for maintaining order on their premises. He suggested ameliorative action and hinted that the building owner, a trust company, might be brought into the discussion if improvements were not made.

The students monitored calls for service at the two apartments after this meeting and found that the previously badly-managed

145

apartment generated an average of 10 calls per month (virtually the same as the well managed apartment) compared with an average of over 150 calls per month prior to the Chief Constable's meeting with the delinquent manager.

Case II[4]

A two-man shoplifting detail became aware of the existence of a number of highly organised shoplifting rings. The shoplifters were stealing merchandise from the city's main retail outlets and exchanging it for cash refunds at the same stores or other branches of the same retail chains. The shoplifting rings were successful in carrying out this operation primarily because the stores' policies regarding cash refunds for returned merchandise varied greatly and were otherwise easy to defeat.

The shoplifting detail explained the situation to police executives, adding that store owners and managers had resisted implementation of suggested improvements for fear of offending legitimate customers, and thus aiding their competitors.

A senior police executive then convened a meeting of all the business owners, managers, and security personnel in the area. The shoplifting detail made a presentation to the meeting, outlining the magnitude of the problem, and illustrating the techniques being used by the shoplifters. The police executive suggested that the stores work in collaboration with the police department to develop a common refund policy. This suggestion was accepted and it was agreed that all the store owners and managers would make a commitment to observe the new policy which would become effective in all the stores on the same day. To accommodate the legitimate concerns of the businessmen in regard to customer relations, the police agreed to mount a media campaign, to coincide with the introduction of the new procedures, which would acquaint the public with the problem and explain why it was necessary for the city's businesses to adopt a uniform and somewhat more stringent refund policy.

At a subsequent meeting of the shoplifting detail and store security personnel, a standard refund policy was developed and taken back to the store owners/managers for approval. The suggested policy was approved and implemented throughout the city on a previously agreed date.   The public relations campaign mounted by the police appeared to be effective, since few shoppers complained to businesses about the new policy. The standard refund policy continues in force and only a few businesses have had to be reminded of their commitment to it.

While the new refund policy may have stimulated the shoplifting rings to devise alternative methods to defraud shopkeepers, the opportunities for fraud inherent in previous policies were effectively reduced.

These cases illustrate how the concept of responsibility can be applied to practical crime problems. From our perspective, the problems were effectively handled because the issues outlined in the theoretical discussion of responsibility were all adequately addressed. Indeed, in each case the process of reassigning responsibility for control of the crimes in question was so well handled that the case histories are deceptively simple. However, let us consider their common elements:

Identification of crime problems

In the first case, the problems were identified by patrol constables. In the second, the problem surfaced through the routine activities of the shoplifting detail. Crime problems can also be identified initially through analysis of offence data, through representations from citizens, business groups or municipal officials, through public attitude and victimisation surveys, and through other sources. The key point is that for the purposes of developing and providing optimally effective crime control strategies, police management and personnel at all levels must make a commitment to systematic analysis of crime problems in the community (Goldstein, 1979).

These cases also illustrate that patrol personnel frequently have a more accurate and detailed knowledge of specific crime problems in the community than senior police administrators (Bittner, 1970; Goldstein, 1979). This observation, in turn, provides one of the bases of recent developments in respect to various forms of 'participatory management' (Task Force on Policing in Ontario, 1974; Wasson, 1975; Basham, 1977; Ministry of the Solicitor General of Canada, 1979), wherein an attempt is made to ensure that the knowledge of police field personnel is effectively incorporated in the identification of crime problems, the analysis of specific crime occurrences, and the development of appropriate crime control strategies. While space limitations preclude a detailed discussion of 'management styles' in policing, it should be clear that the perspective offered here could be most readily applied in police departments which have adopted one or another variant of 'participatory management'.

Detailed analysis of specific crime occurrences

In the case of the apartment buildings, a rigorous analysis of the crime problem was undertaken. With limited operational resources, the Chief Constable, at no cost to the taxpayers, wisely made use of research skills in a neighbouring community. In the second case, the constables on the shoplifting detail analysed the problem and suggested an appropriate solution.

Most police departments have developed, in varying degrees, a capacity for sophisticated analysis of crime problems. With increasing frequency, crime specific analyses are being used as a basis for developing enforcement strategies. To a lesser extent such analyses are also being used to develop prevention strategies. However, here it appears that the results are most frequently interpreted within the context of traditional police responses.

This is not surprising, since police administrators have not typically been expected or required to re-examine traditional police responses to specific crime problems, to explore alternative solutions to crime problems, or to evaluate rigorously the effects of enforcement or prevention practices. Indeed, where increasing emphasis has been placed on the role of the police in crime prevention, many police departments have adopted a variety of 'packaged' crime prevention programmes without undertaking a careful analysis of the nature, extent, or salience of the crime problems in their communities. Programmes such as 'operation identification', 'neighbourhood watch', and others are no doubt effective in varying degrees in preventing crime, improving police-community relations, promoting a sense of 'community', and mobilising a wide range of community resources to control crime. On the other hand, these packaged programmes are frequently assumed to be effective and are introduced without having first determined the magnitude or seriousness of the crime problem to which the 'prescription' is addressed. The presumed effectiveness of these packaged programmes likewise militates against their evaluation (Campbell, 1969).

While the introduction of packaged programmes may be justified under the assumption that the circumstances surrounding the occurrence of certain crimes are sufficiently similar in different communities, we recommend that evidence of this similarity be assembled before introducing any programme. Even if there were persuasive evidence of programme effectiveness, the problem to which it is addressed may not be sufficiently serious in particular communities to create and sustain the interest necessary to implement and maintain the programme and justify its cost.

Unless the programmes to be implemented derive from a rigorous evaluation of community crime problems, a fundamental re-examination of the locus of responsibility for specific crime problems, and a broadly directed search for alternative solutions, they can be faddish, wasteful, ineffective, and at worst, militate against police administrators developing increasingly effective crime control strategies by giving the appearance, to themselves and to the community, that effective crime control programmes are already in place.

Determining levels of responsibility for crime occurrence and crime control

Before deciding upon an appropriate police-community response to the specific crime problems discussed above, the police examined the problems from the point of view of determing who in the community shared responsibility for the occurrences of the crimes and who, individually or collectively, had some level of competence to deal with them. In each case, the police were looking for the broadest possible range of solutions to the specific crime problems, and were guided by the philosophy that, wherever possible, expensive, highly trained police resources would be employed only with respect to crime problems which were beyond the competence of others in the community to handle. Moreover, the police were guided by the view that, where possible, their role should be that of catalyst, negotiating to have action taken by those with some responsibility and competence to control the crimes in question.

As the case histories illustrate, the assessment of competence or potential competence must be balanced by consideration of social values other than crime control. The police did not attempt, for example, to have the building manager in *Case I* institute security procedures which would have caused undue inconvenience to the tenants in the building. Nor did the police in *Case II* attempt to have procedures implemented which would have unreasonably infringed upon consumer or corporate interests.

In addition, the cases illustrate why it is not possible to determine levels of competence, responsibility, or accountability for crime control in the abstract. It is clearly unreasonable to make such determinations except in reference to specific crime occurrences.

Thus, in the absence of empirical analyses of the sort required, we cannot, with confidence, make assertions about the extent to which the application of the perspective adopted here will contribute to a reduction in the incidence of crimes of violence. On the other hand, extrapolating from the theoretical discussion, case studies (only two of which are cited here), and the existing literature, it is clear that this perspective holds enormous potential for reducing the incidence of non-violent property crime. Transferring responsibility to the 'organised and well managed sector of the community' (Heywood, 1979b)[5] is likely to be particularly effective in this regard, since negotiating agreements and securing accountability is facilitated by the existence of numerous pressures and sanctions which can legitimately be employed.

The present or potential competence of others in the community to prevent or deter non-violent property crime is of particular importance here since these offences consume an enormous amount of police resources and contribute to the view, shared by what we suspect to be a growing number of policemen, that they are simply working for the insurance companies (Shearing, 1974). Even slight shifts in responsibility for dealing with such occurrences should, over time, substantially reduce demands for police service. This in turn could facilitate the gradual redeployment of police resources towards those offences and offenders that are demonstrably beyond the competence of the community to control (Heywood, 1979b). This might include strengthening investigations aimed at arresting known offenders and, in more general ways, applying the philosophy advanced herein to the prevention of economic and white collar crime (Grant, 1979).

As discussed above, it is only recently that notions of joint responsibility or levels of responsibility have gained currency in developing responses to crime problems, and some police, citizens, and businesses are likely to resist a shift in the locus of responsibility for specific crime problems (Ericson and MacFarlane, 1976; Guyot, 1977; Heywood, 1979b).

This resistance may be particularly evident in police departments since what is required is a radical restructuring of police expectations about the nature of policing. Consider, for example, the following comment on the extent to which many police personnel, in North America at least, feel wedded to their patrol cars.

> Since the radio is the source of most 'action', the predisposition of most officers matches this need for them to be 'in service' (i.e., available to respond to calls for service). Thus, in a strange twist of language, an officer is 'in service' when driving aimlessly about and 'out of service' when dealing with citizens. As a result, the priority for the officer is to be free of citizen contact as rapidly as possible in order to again be 'in service'. (The Police Foundation, 1978, pp. 70–1).

Given the pervasiveness of this view, it is not surprising that police administrators who have attempted to restructure their departments have experienced difficulty (Basham, 1977; Parkinson, 1977; Kelling and Wycoff, 1978; Wycoff and Kelling, 1978).

Restructuring public expectations is no less difficult and at least as time consuming. By focusing on specific crimes, however, police may be able to effect numerous small shifts in the expectations of specific social units. Although they do not deal directly with public expectations in regard to crime control, the results of an analysis of response time (Pate, et al., 1977) are encouraging in this regard. Here it was suggested that public expectations could be altered so as to conform more closely to reality, and that this shift in expectations may well have a positive effect in terms of public satisfaction with the delivery of police services. Similarly, studies of alternative ways of handling calls for service also show that expectations can be moulded (Gay, 1977; Birmingham Police Department, 1979; Farmer and Furstenberg, 1979). A carefully planned programme of meetings with appropriate community groups, business groups and political officials for the purpose of promulgating the police department's philosophy within the community would help to maintain balance between police and public expectations.

The notion of balance is crucial. Experience has shown that police executives who get too far ahead of their subordinates or the community they serve may find themselves in search of employment (Kelling and Wycoff, 1978; Wycoff and Kelling, 1978).

Negotiating and enforcing an agreement

As outlined in the theoretical discussion and illustrated in the cases cited above, it is necessary to negotiate the transfer of responsibility for specific crime problems and to establish some means for ensuring appropriate action. It is most unlikely that the group or corporate body to whom responsibility is being shifted will immediately acknowledge that their property or operations are generating a substantial strain on police resources, accept that they have a duty, up to their level of competence, for the control of specific crimes, and take appropriate action. In our view, the failure of many well intentioned and theoretically sound community based crime control efforts can be attributed to the absence of some means for ensuring that the members of the community involved accepted and effectively discharged their responsibility.

In addition to the sound empirical basis for negotiation developed through the rigorous analysis of specific crime problems, there are numerous other pressures which police can legitimately bring into these discussions (National Crime Prevention Institute, 1978; see also Shearing and Leon, 1977). Apart from hinting that profit minded property owners would be brought into the negotiations (which was enough to secure compliance in *Case I*) and moral persuasion (which was used to good effect in *Case II*), most communities have an assortment of by-laws, licensing provisions, permits, regulations, and related legal instruments which can legitimately be invoked, if necessary, to ensure co-operation.

The City of Oakland, California, for example, has a bye-law under which business owners can be required by the police to adopt specific technological aids to increase the security of their buildings and contents. The mere threat of applying the bye-law is usually enough to secure compliance.[6] The situation is likely to be similar in other cities and for other potential sanctions which the police could impose or have imposed by appropriate city officials. Whether 'new forms of authority' (Goldstein, 1979) would be necessary to negotiate and enforce some types of agreements remains an interesting empirical question.

Implications for research

In order to develop optimally effective crime control strategies, it is necessary to identify and analyse community crime problems; to examine, in detail, how particular crimes are carried out; to conduct a thorough examination of who in the community has contributed to the existence of the crime problem in question; and to examine, in depth, the full range of community resources which could potentially be mobilised to control the specific crime.

Clearly, there is much scope here for innovative research and analysis by researchers, in or outside of government, and by police research and planning units. One of the principal advantages of this approach to crime control is that by treating the assignment of responsibility and community competence for crime control as problematic, there is a high potential for bringing research into a much closer relationship with significant policy and operational concerns (Engstad, 1975).

Another advantage of research which focuses on specific crime problems is the fact that the results, as illustrated in the evaluation of Seattle's Community Crime Prevention Program (Cirel, et al., 1977), are likely to be specific and identifiable (Goldstein, 1979). In addition, the implications of research results, whether in respect to policy or operations, will be less ambiguous than those deriving from macro-analyses of the effects of police resources on crime, analyses of the effects of police functions on crime, or analyses of the effects of specific programmes on more global categories of crime such as robbery, theft, or arson (Goldstein, 1979).

Moreover, because this perspective is both concrete and practical, and because it is a logical extension of existing police crime analysis capabilities, it is probable that the police will be more accommodating of research and more likely to make use of research findings.[7] Finally, because this approach calls for crime specific research to figure prominently in the development of crime control policies and strategies, and not simply in their evaluation, research arising out of this perspective should, by design, generate numerous constructive suggestions for police, policy makers, legislators, the public, and others concerned with crime control.

Suggestions for research

Numerous concrete suggestions for research arise out of the perspective adopted in this paper. These include, but are by no means limited to:

1   Research directed toward developing and refining methods of crime specific analysis which would include an examination of opportunities for the occurrence of the crime in question together with an analysis of who, individually or collectively, is contributing to the existence of the specific crime problem. Studies of this sort would provide an empirical basis for the development of enforcement or prevention strategies, while stimulating a search for the broadest possible range of alternative solutions to specific crime problems.

2   Research aimed at determining the existing or potential competence of the broadest spectrum of social units, including the police, individuals, businesses, and others to control the occurrence of specific crimes. Studies of this sort would provide an empirical basis for making decisions in respect to the assignment or transference of responsibility for crime control.

3   Research examining public and police expectations in regard to their respective levels of responsibility for specific aspects of crime control. These studies would provide baseline data against which shifts in expectations could be measured over time.

4   Studies of the processes by which the assignment or transference of responsibility for the control of specific crimes are negotiated, and the effectiveness of the pressures or sanctions which can legitimately be invoked to enforce compliance. These studies would contribute to the development of strategies for the successful negotiation and maintenance of specific crime control strategies.

5   Studies aimed at evaluating the effectiveness of crime specific enforcement or prevention strategies, together with studies which assess the generalisability of those strategies found to be successful. For those crime control strategies that are generalisable, the effect of widespread adoption of these techniques could be simulated for the dual purposes of

assessing their potential for crime control in the community and for projecting the cost effectiveness associated with their widespread implementation.

6   Research directed toward the development of productivity and performance measures and reward structures which are responsive to the supporting organisational forms and innovative preventive policing practices arising out of this perspective (Police Foundation, 1978; Heywood, 1979b).

7   Comparative analyses of shifts in responsibility for crime control (community resources, private security) with shifts in responsibility in the areas of corrections (community-based residential centres, day parole), the courts (diversion, restitution), and in areas outside the criminal justice system (notably health care). Studies examining these trends could prove helpful in improving criminal justice system functioning and coordination, while increasing understanding of the criminal justice system within a broad social context.

8   Research focusing on the crime generating potential of new technology and business practices, together with studies directed toward assessing the level of responsibility and competence of legislators and policy makers to develop policies and take positive action toward reducing the crime generating potential (and potential burden on the police and others in the community) inherent in these developments.

9   Research directed toward an assessment of the adequacy of existing police powers (Goldstein, 1979), the powers of municipalities, and the powers of diverse regulatory agencies for ensuring that responsibility for crime control, either through reducing the crime generating potential of technological and other advances or through direct crime prevention, can be meaningfully assigned and enforced.

10 Historical research on the effects of shifts in police responsibility for crime control on police organisation, management, and relations with the community.

Implications for criminal justice policy

Most western societies share a broad conception of criminal justice which is based on principles of equity, due process, and humane treatment, and the institutions which have been established to handle criminal justice concerns typically have stated objectives which embrace these broad principles. However, it is a common observation that the operational policies of the components of the criminal justice system

154

do not always adequately reflect these first principles and too often are antagonistic to them.

Moreover, since most operational policies are developed by the relatively autonomous components of the criminal justice system in response to day to day problems, these policies are rarely integrated with those of other criminal justice institutions, and are as likely to serve the bureaucracy as the objectives the institution was established to achieve.

Given these difficulties, there is now considerable interest in the development of a criminal justice policy which would, in Banton's words (1978, p.3), encompass 'the most appropriate strategy for reducing crime and promoting the public peace'. This formulation has the enormous advantage of not equating criminal justice policy with criminal justice system policy. It promotes explicit consideration of the role of the broader community in crime control.

This call for an end to the relative isolation of the police and the other criminal justice system components from the larger community acknowledges the pressures enumerated earlier which are forcing a re-examination of the role of the police and community in crime control. The position developed here is that these pressures are a positive force which can be exploited to generate crime control policies which follow from basic social values and are, at the same time, more effective than the common practice of simply passing the problem on to the police.

As will be clear by now, we do not believe that arguments from first principles are likely to be very productive in this regard. Rather, we think that more is to be gained, at least initially, by approaching the problem from the perspective of the specific analysis of quite narrowly defined behaviours, the responsibility for which is apportioned according to the level of competence which can be established in various sectors of society. From this perspective the policy which would emerge would be empirically grounded and operationally meaningful, and more importantly, it would be a policy concerning not just the police or other criminal justice system components, but rather the entire community.

A criminal policy which is sensitive to the ideas of responsibility and competence developed here would also make it clear that legislators, policy planners, and other officials have responsibilities for crime control. Since the focus of this paper has been on policing, we have not stressed the role of these other groups. Nonetheless, since their failure to carry out their responsibilities frequently translates into increased demands on the police, it is worth elaborating somewhat on the role these groups should play in reducing the potential for new forms of crime occasioned by technological innovations

155

or new business practices.

To take a retrospective example, consider the introduction of credit cards and the consequent enormous volume of fraudulent credit card transactions with which the police have had to cope. Credit cards were distributed to the public with insufficient regard for the potential contribution to existing community crime problems inherent in their mode of distribution or the manner of their use. As a result, cards were distributed with almost reckless abandon and accepted in payment for goods or services often without verification of either the card or the person using it. At least some of the costs inherent in the proliferation of fraudulent credit card transactions occasioned by these developments have been passed on to the tax-payer and the consumer, who through the provision of police services, have been forced to provide a subsidy to credit card companies and the businesses using them. It is clear that the corporations which introduced credit cards, government regulatory bodies, and the businesses using credit cards did not adequately meet their responsibilities for crime control by providing reasonable safeguards which could have prevented widespread abuse.

One of the problems with such innovations is that the technology changes so rapidly that the police are forced to spend an inordinate amount of their resources devising new apprehension and prevention strategies. Thus, to take one further example, micro-processors now available will soon make it possible to control access to bank accounts and data banks by means of speech recognition devices. Given current conceptions of corporate and governmental responsibility, such devices will be designed and implemented with considerable tolerance in order to avoid offending legitimate users. This, of course, will mean that illegitimate users will have less difficulty defeating the systems and many of the costs of such fraudulent use will again be passed on to the taxpayer through increased demands on the police.

As these examples illustrate, the criminal justice policy which we envisage would not be a policy whose application would be the sole responsibility of criminal justice agencies. Rather, the policies which would emerge through the application of the perspective offered here would place specific responsibilities on a broad range of social units, not least the policy planners, regulatory agency personnel, and the legislators who should ultimately be accountable for policy.

Conclusion

The police are only one of numerous social agencies, institutions, businesses, and other formal or informal social units, which, together with individual citizens, have a responsibility and a capacity to contribute to crime control. In the preceeding discussion, we have taken the position that police effectiveness in crime control can best be conceptualised and examined within this broad context.

By linking recent developments in crime-specific analysis with the concept of responsibility, we have provided both a conceptual framework and empirical basis for such an examination. The merits of this perspective derive from the fact that it can be constructively applied, through research, to the solution of practical problems facing the police as well as to the development of crime control policies by all levels of government.

Finally, if this perspective were applied to the more numerous non-crime related demands for police service, responsibility and accountability for handling these problems could likewise be apportioned according to the levels of competence which could be established in other, more appropriate, components of the community. Relieving the police of much of the responsibility for handling non-crime related problems would greatly enlarge the pool of police resources available for handling those aspects of crime control and other problems with which the police are uniquely competent to deal.

Notes

1 The authors are particularly indebted to Superintendent R. Heywood (Royal Canadian Mounted Police) and Professor Alan Grant (Osgoode Hall Law School) for their contribution to the development of many of the ideas presented in this paper, to Tony Pate, of the Police Foundation, and our colleagues in the Ministry who commented on earlier drafts of this paper. Naturally, they cannot be held accountable for what we have done with their experiences, insights, and suggestions. The views expressed in this paper are our own and do not necessarily reflect the views of the Solicitor General of Canada.
2 Our use of the phrase 'responsibility for crime occurrence' rarely implies a legal responsibility. In most cases some degree of responsibility for crime occurrence and control can be assigned to those who create opportunities or incentives for crime or fail to take reasonable precautions to reduce inviting opportunities for crime. As noted earlier, in some jurisdictions acts of commission or ommission of this sort may be defined as legal responsibilities.
3 This case study derives from discussions with Superintendent Heywood and is referred to in Heywood (1979b). Readers, particularly those with experience in policing, are no doubt familiar with numerous similar cases.

4 This case derives from discussions with Deputy Chief R. Steward (Vancouver City Police). See Parkinson (1977) for a thorough examination of related developments within the Vancouver Police Department.

5 It is not possible within the confines of this paper to examine adequately the implications of our analysis for the future development of 'in house' and 'contract' security services. It is clear, however, that the shift of responsibility for certain aspects of crime control to corporations is likely to expand further the role and influence of the private security community (Shearing and Farnell, 1979; Stenning and Shearing, 1979; Williams, 1974).

6 In a recent discussion with a member of the Oakland Police Department's Community Services Unit, the authors were advised that CSU personnel are able to secure compliance in 95 per cent of cases without enforcement of the bye-laws. Interestingly, the CSU has also adopted a 'False Alarm Abatement Program' in which CSU officers advise business owners/managers that once they exceed a pre-determined number of false alarms, the police will no longer respond to calls. This assignment of responsibility appears to have reduced false alarms and the attendant drain on police resources by 40 per cent. Montreal, Quebec, and Fredericton, New Brunswick, have bye-laws which enable the police to bill the alarm owner for costs incurred in responding to false alarms.

7 Wilson (1976, p. 7) has noted that: 'Of all parts of the Criminal Justice System with which I am familiar, the greatest receptiveness to innovation, research change, and planned experiments has been the police component. This is not to say that all police departments are open to these attitudes, but of those parts of the Criminal Justice System as a whole that are amenable to change and research, the police are substantially over represented'. In our view, Wilson's observations apply equally in Canada. Regrettably, recent developments in Canadian policing, many of which reflect an application of the ideas which are central to this paper, are not well documented in the literature. With a number of notable exceptions (for example, Parkinson, 1973; Heywood, 1979b) developments in the field are proceeding more rapidly than they are in the literature on Canadian policing.

References

Banton, M., (1978), 'Crime prevention in the context of criminal justice policy', *Police Studies,* June.

Basham, G., (1977), *A Planning Implementation and Organization Theory Guide to the Team Policing Model,* British Columbia Justice Development Commission, Victoria, BC.

Birmingham Police Department, (1979), 'An Analysis of Citizen Attitudes to Police Response: The Birmingham Experiment', Birmingham, Alabama; (unpublished).

Bittner, E., (1970), *The Functions of the Police in Modern Society,* Department of Health, Education and Welfare, (HSM) 73-9072, Washington, DC.

Blackmore, J., (1979), 'Focusing on the victim', *Police Magazine,* March, pp. 24—37.

Bottomley, A. K., and Coleman, C., (1976), 'Criminal statistics: the police role in the discovery and detection of crime', *International Journal of Criminology and Penology,* 4, pp.33—58.

Campbell, D. T., (1969), 'Reforms as experiments', *American Psychologist,* 24, pp. 409—29.

Canada, Revised Statutes, (1970), *The Criminal Code,* chapter C-34, section 118, para. (b), Queen's Printer, Ottawa, Ont.

Chaiken, J. M., Lawless, M. W., and Stevenson, K. A., (1975), *The Impact of Police Activities on Crime: Robberies in the New York City Subway System,* The Rand Corporation, Santa Monica, Calif.

Chaiken, J. M., (1976), 'What is known about the deterrent effects of police activities', in Cramer, J. A. (ed.), *Preventing Crime,* Sage Publications, Beverly Hills, Calif.

Chelimksy, E., (1977), 'Improving the use of evaluation: an agency perspective', *Prison Journal,* 57, pp. 13—18.

Cirel, P., Evans, P., McGillis, D., and Whitcomb, D., (1977), *Community Crime Prevention Program: Seattle, Washington,* NILECJ, Washington, DC.

Clarke, R. V. G., and Heal, K. H., (1979), 'Police effectiveness in dealing with crime: some current British research', *The Police Journal,* 52, pp. 24—41.

Clarke, R. V. G., (1977), 'Psychology and crime', *Bulletin of the British Psychological Society,* 30, pp. 280—3.

Coates, J., (1974), 'A future perspective', *Community Crime Prevention and the Local Official,* Office of Urban Services, Washington, DC.

Critchley, T. A., (1967), *A History of Police in England and Wales: 1900-1966,* Constable, London.

Engstad, P., (1975), 'Environmental opportunities and the ecology of crime', in Silverman, R., and Teevan, J. J., Jr., (eds.), *Crime in Canadian Society*, Butterworths, Scarborough, Ont.

Engstad, P., and Lioy, M., (eds.), (1979), *Proceedings: Workshop on Police Productivity and Performance*, Solicitor General of Canada, Ottawa, Ont.

Ericson, R. V., and MacFarlane, P. D., (1976), 'The Police and Legal Change', Ministry of Transport, Ottawa, Ont., (unpublished manuscript).

Farmer, M. T., (1976), 'Direct Crime Prevention: A State of the Art', Police Foundation, Washington, DC., (unpublished manuscript).

Farmer, M. T., and Furstenberg, M., (1979), *Alternative Strategies for Responding to Police Calls for Service*, Police Executive Research Forum, Washington, DC.

Gay, W., (1977), *Improving Patrol Productivity*, Law Enforcement Assistance Administration, Washington, DC.

Goldstein, H., (1979), 'Improving policing: a problem-oriented approach', *Crime and Delinquency*, 25, pp. 236—58.

Grant, A., (1979), 'Some philosophical, political, policy and operational concerns in the delivery of police services', in Engstad, P., and Lioy, M., (eds.), *Proceedings: Workshop on Police Productivity and Performance*, Solicitor General of Canada, Ottawa, Ont.

Greenwood, P. W., and Petersilia, J., (1975), *The Criminal Investigative Process, Volume I, Summary and Policy Implications*, The Rand Corporation, Santa Monica, Calif.

Guyct, D., (1977), 'The organisation of police departments', *Criminal Justice Abstracts*, 9, pp. 231—56.

Henig, J., Lineberry, R. L., and Milner, N. A., (1977), 'The policy impact of policy evaluation: some implications of the Kansas City Patrol Experiment', in Gardiner, J., (ed.), *Public Law and Public Policy*, Praeger, New York.

Heywood, R., (1979a), 'Traditional and innovative policing', in Engstad, P., and Lioy, M., (eds.), *Proceedings: Workshop on Police Productivity and Performance*, Solicitor General of Canada, Ottawa, Ont.

Heywood, R., (1979b), 'Keynote Address', *Proceedings: National Symposium on Preventive Policing*, Solicitor General of Canada, Ottawa, Ont., (in press).

Home Office (Crime Policy Planning Unit) (1978), 'Report of the Working Group on Crime Prevention, Home Office, London, mimeo.

Kelling, G. L., (1978), 'Police field services and crime: the presumed effects of a capacity', *Crime and Delinquency*, 24, pp. 173—84.

Kelling, G. L., Pate, T., Dieckman, D., and Brown, C. E., (1974), *The Kansas City Preventive Patrol Experiment*, Police Foundation,

Washington, DC.

Kelling, G. L., and Wycoff, M. A., (1978), *The Dallas Experience: Human Resources Development*, Police Foundation, Washington, DC.

Kelly, W. H., (1965), 'The police', in McGrath, W. T., (ed.), *Crime and its Treatment in Canada*, MacMillan of Canada, Toronto, Ont.

Krajick, K., (1978), 'Does patrol prevent crime?', *Police Magazine*, 1, pp. 4—16.

Letkeman, P., (1973), *Crime as Work*, Prentice-Hall, Englewood Cliffs, NJ.

Lynn, L. E. Jr. (ed.), (1978), *Knowledge and Policy: The Uncertain Connection*, National Academy of Sciences, Washington, DC.

Manning, P. K., (1971), 'The police: mandate, strategies and appearance', in Douglas, J. (ed.), *Crime and Justice in American Society*, Bobs—Merrill,

Manning, P. K., (1977), *Police Work: The Social Organisation of Policing*, The MIT Press, Cambridge, Mass.

Mehay, S., and Furlong, W. J., (1978), 'The deterrent effect of urban police services: empirical results for Canada', paper presented at Southern Economic Association, Washington, DC, November, (mimeo).

Mayhew, P., Clarke, R. V. G., Burrows, J. N., Hough, J. M., and Winchester, S. W. C., (1978), *Crime in Public View*, Home Office Research Study, no. 49, HMSO, London.

Meuser, P., (1976), *An Assessment of the Burnaby RCMP Project Operation Identification*, British Columbia Police Commission, Vancouver, BC.

Ministry of the Solicitor General of Canada, (1979), *Proceedings: National Symposium on Preventive Policing*, Solicitor General of Canada, Ottawa, Ont., (in press).

Murphy, P., (1974), 'The police perspective', *Community Crime Prevention and the Local Official*, Office of Urban Services, Washington, DC.

National Advisory Commission on Criminal Justice Standards and Goals, (1973), *Community Crime Prevention*, US Government Printing Office, Washington, DC.

National Crime Prevention Institute (1978), *Understanding Crime Prevention*, NCPI Press, Lexington, Ky.

Oakland Municipal Code (1969), Article 12, Section 3-12.08 to 3-12.22.

Office of Urban Services (1974), *Community Crime Prevention and the Local Official*, Office of Urban Services, Washington, DC.

Ontario, Revised Statutes (1974), The Police Act, Chapter 351:2(5), Queen's Printer, Toronto, Ont.

161

Parkinson, G., (1977), *Figuring It Out,* British Columbia Justice Development Commission, Victoria, BC.

Pate, T., Ferrera, A., Bowers, R. A., and Lorence, J., (1976), *Police Response Time: Its Determinants and Effects,* Police Foundation, Washington, DC.

Police Foundation (1978), 'Police Roles and their Future for Organizational Structuring', a response to the NILECJ request for a research proposal (unpublished).

Province of Ontario (1974), *Task Force on Policing in Ontario,* Queen's Printer, Toronto, Ont.

Reppetto, T.,(1974), *Residential Crime,* Ballinger, Cambridge, Mass.

Robinson, M. P., (1977), *Reintroducing Community Responsibility,* British Columbia Police Commission, Vancouver, BC.

Shearing, C. C., (1974), 'Dial-a-cop: a study of police mobilization', in Akers, R., and Sagarin, E. (eds.), *Crime Prevention and Social Control,* Praeger, New York.

Shearing, C. D., and Leon, J., (1977), 'Reconsidering the police role: a challenge to a challenge of popular conception', *Canadian Journal of Criminology and Corrections,* 19, pp. 331-45.

Shearing, C. D., and Farnell, M., (1979), *Policing for Profit,* University of Toronto Press, Toronto, Ont., (in press).

Stenning, P., and Shearing, C. D., (1979), *Search and Seizure Powers of Private Security Personnel,* National Law Reform Commission of Canada, (in press).

Trojanowicz, R. C., and Moss, F. M., (1975), 'Crime prevention through citizen involvement', *Police Chief,* 42, pp. 66–71.

Waller, I., and Okihiro, N., (1978), *Burglary and the Public,* University of Toronto Press, Toronto, Ont.

Wasson, D. K., (1977), *Community-Based Preventive Policing: A Review,* Solicitor General of Canada, Ottawa, Ont.

Williams, D. G. T., (1974), 'Crime prevention and private security: problems of control and responsibility', *The Australian Law Journal,* 48, pp. 380–7.

Wilson, J. Q., (1974), 'Do the police prevent crime?', *New York Times Magazine,* 6 October.

Wilson, J. Q., (1975), *Thinking about Crime,* Basic Books, New York.

Wilson, J. Q., (1976), 'Coping with crime', *Criminal Justice Review,* 1, pp. 1–12.

Wilson, J. Q., and Boland, B., (1978), 'The effect of the police on crime', *Law and Society,* 12, pp. 367–90.

Wycoff, M. A., and Kelling, G. L., (1978), *The Dallas Experience: Organizational Reform,* Police Foundation, Washington, DC.

162

Subject index

Detection rates—see clear-up
rates
Devon and Cornwall
Constabulary, 13
Discretion, 8, 21, 104–118

Effectiveness
CID—see investigations
citizen satisfaction, 10, 52
clear-up rates as measure,
84
defined, viii-x, 2, 17, 61,
70–72, 99, 117, 143–144
efficiency and effectiveness,
ix, 3, 17
measures of, 36, 51
patrol—see patrol
recorded crime rates, 70–94
reported crime, 52, 53
response time—see response
time
unrelated to resource levels,
141
Expenditure on Police, vii, 46,
141, 142

Fear of crime, 9, 13, 134
Forensic services, 19, 29, 37

Home Office, 1, 89, 139, 140
Home Office Research Unit, 1
Houston Police Department, 45

Integrated Criminal Apprehensions Program, 42
Investigations
and clear-up—see clear-up rates
arrest rates, 36–37, 42
case-screening, 37, 40, 41, 60,
127, 128
'indirect detections', 89–93
offences taken into consideration, 5, 6, 89–93
by patrol officers, 39, 41, 128,
129

preparation of evidence, 37–38
by specialist teams, 133
source of detection, 87, 91–
93
team policing, 40, 59, 129–134
time spent on administration,
37, 42
in Utrecht, 133
victim satisfaction, 38, 41

Kansas City Prevention Patrol
Experiment, xi, 4, 18, 29, 49,
58, 60, 73, 130, 139

Law Enforcement Assistance
Administration, (LEAA), 4, 41,
42

Metonymy vs metaphor, 105,
108–110
Ministry of Solicitor General,
Canada, 147

National Association for the Care
and Resettlement of Offenders,
(NACRO), 13
New York Police Department,
4, 27, 28, 56
National Institute of Law Enforce-
ment and Criminal Justice,
(NILECJ), 4, 17, 23, 25, 29,
30, 35, 39, 40
'No-crimes', 79–81

Offences taken into consideration—
see 'TICs'
'Operation 25', 27

Patrol
arrest-oriented, 58–59
community-oriented, 21, 58, 59
directed (aggressive), 57, 58
high-visibility, 21
location-oriented, 21

164

Name index